Managing in Organisations

Managing in Organisations is a concise, access~~~ ~~~~~~~~ ~~ ~~~ ~~~ ~~ the difficult job of line management. It offers a kit of management tools and a range of worked examples that can be used to address the key tasks that managers face in the workplace. This book provides clear insights into how people behave everyday in real organisations. The fundamentals of key theories and sources are covered throughout for those coming to the subject for the first time.

Topics covered include individual, group, and team organisational behaviour; organisational culture and diversity; supervision and leadership; organisational design; management and change; and governance. This book considers small and larger enterprises as well as public, private, and third sectors. Short cases link the issues in the chapter and provide opportunities for developing skills and discussion.

This book provides an introduction to the world of managing in organisations and is suitable for those who study organisational behaviour, organisational studies, management, and human resource management. It will also be very useful to the entrepreneur planning a small start-up and to the busy manager of a small- or medium-sized enterprise seeking to understand how best to manage the organisation for performance.

Tom Elsworth is a senior lecturer teaching Organisational Behaviour, Leadership, General Management, and Strategic Management at Oxford Brookes Business School. He has 50 years of experience in management at all levels, including 25 years in industry and then 25 years in academia. In 2024, Tom published his first book, *Understanding Strategic Analysis*, published by Routledge.

Managing in Organisations

A Practical Guide

Tom Elsworth

Routledge
Taylor & Francis Group

LONDON AND NEW YORK

First published 2025
by Routledge
4 Park Square, Milton Park, Abingdon, Oxon OX14 4RN

and by Routledge
605 Third Avenue, New York, NY 10158

Routledge is an imprint of the Taylor & Francis Group, an informa business

British Library Cataloguing-in-Publication Data
A catalogue record for this book is available from the British Library

ISBN: 9781032686578 (hbk)
ISBN: 9781032686615 (pbk)
ISBN: 9781032686592 (ebk)

DOI: 10.4324/9781032686592

Typeset in Baskerville
by codeMantra

Contents

Acknowledgements

I would like to acknowledge the contribution to this book of my wife, Jane. She very kindly spent a good deal of time reading through my work, advising me, and suggesting improvements and corrections. I have also benefitted greatly from the support of my colleagues Drs Uma Urs and Shirley Velasquez-Hoque who also read through the whole thing and offered many words of guidance.

Any errors or infelicities remaining are entirely my own fault.

1 Introduction

A PRACTICAL APPROACH TO LINE MANAGEMENT

Managing in Organisations sets out a practical approach to the difficult job of line managing in organisations. It offers guidance and tools that can be used to address most of the tasks that face the manager in leading and directing the team, department, or division of the organisation for which they are responsible. It does not cover tasks properly dealt with by specialist Human Resources Management books such as recruitment, discipline, and grievances. Equally, it does not cover functional management responsibilities such as operations, finance, budgeting, and marketing. Neither does it cover the tasks involved in the general management of the organisation such as strategy development or issues around governance.

The guidance and tools offered here are explained in this book in terms of a straightforward view of how people behave in organisations. The academic theory behind this, known as organisational behaviour, is outlined in a later chapter, also giving indications to the interested reader as to where they could learn more by reading in greater depth.

MANAGING PEOPLE IS DIFFICULT

The main idea underlying *Managing in Organisations* is that the organisations in question are made up of range of resources such as finance, equipment, and property but that these resources are easy to manage compared with the management of people, the most significant resource of any organisation, management of which is not at all easy.

DOI: 10.4324/9781032686592-1

People have a mind of their own, and they will, always, on all occasions, use it to some degree or other. Indeed, as managers, we certainly want our colleagues to have their own minds and to use them, imaginatively, in the best interests of the organisation. Thus, the fundamental key to organisational management is to know how to deal with people such that they put out their best efforts on behalf of the organisation.

Managing in Organisations covers key ideas about individual, group, and team organisational behaviour; organisational culture; and the intersection of culture with issues around diversity and inclusion. It also covers the applications of these ideas in supervision and team leadership, organisational design, the role of power and internal politics, and the management of change. The idea underlying *Managing in Organisations* is that a focused knowledge of organisational behaviour is both necessary and sufficient to enable a good practical job to be done of line managing in any organisation, whether big or small. Line management is tough, but straightforward techniques exist to ease the process.

THE STRUCTURE OF MANAGING IN ORGANISATIONS

In addition to the topic-specific content of each chapter, as set out in this section, each of Chapters 4–9 includes one of a diverse set of short cases designed to link to the chapters and offer questions, for individual learning or class discussion, tackling use of each of the tools and methods in the chapter. The cases are typically around one page in length, and each is based on a different sector and organisational type including public, private, and third sector, both large and small. The scenarios have been chosen to be well known to the general business reader such as hotel, retail, airline, and automotive. These cases have been written specifically for *Managing in Organisations* and are based on published sources or the author's own practice.

In addition, each chapter includes a worked example to demonstrate applications of the ideas in the chapter. All of these are set in the same imaginary organisation (see "Motorsport Engineering Ltd" section) which is undertaking large-scale change following major concern over declining business performance and a subsequent review of strategy. This situation requires the change manager and line managers throughout the organisation to reconsider what they do and how they do it, thereby offering the opportunity for all the topics covered in *Managing in Organisations* to be looked at in detail.

- **Chapter 2 – Management** – deals with management as a general topic, distinguishing between distinct types of management and identifying those covered by the following chapters of this book. It also addresses several key topics around the skills and day-to-day activities of successful managers.

- **Chapter 3 Organisational Behaviour, Leadership, and Management of Change in perspective** – Deals with the overall theoretical background to the development of understanding of these fields of management. It indicates the additional reading that would lead to a greater depth of theoretical understanding.
- **Chapter 4 Understanding Individual Behaviour** – Deals with the origin of individual behaviour via the study of motivation, leading to the development of a practical approach to motivation of use to leaders at all levels in organisations.
- **Chapter 5 Understanding Group and Team Behaviour** – Deals with the formation of groups and teams from a collection of individuals, how these collective entities behave, and how to cope with the opportunities and problems which they throw up.
- **Chapter 6 Organisational Design** – Deals with different approaches to the design and structuring of organisations and how these may be appropriate to the circumstances prevailing, with a view to enabling informed choices to be made about initiating or changing the design of organisations.
- **Chapter 7 Emergent Properties of Organisations; Culture, Power, and Politics** – Deals with the reality of organisations which is that they are human societies and, therefore, exhibit all the characteristics of any society. Specifically, the chapter deals with organisational culture which is often the single largest factor in organisational success and failure, the use and abuse of organisational internal power and the political behaviour used to acquire and deploy power.
- **Chapter 8 Leadership** – Deals with practical guidance for the leader in the context of leadership as another automatic consequence of human society. There are many theories of leadership, outlined in Chapter 2, but this chapter adopts none of them per se, relying on organisational experience.
- **Chapter 9 The Manager as Leader of Change** – Deals with change as the biggest management challenge facing organisational leaders both in terms of the difficulty of achieving success and the continuous nature of the task. A toolkit for practical change is set out for use by the reader.
- **Chapter 10 Worked Case Study** – Offers a worked example in addition to that in each chapter to demonstrate applications of the ideas in the chapter set in a different imaginary organisation and situation and set in a different sector.

AN INTERVIEW WITH REBECCA RAWNSLEY – A CAREER IN MODERN MANAGEMENT

Most of the chapters include material drawn from an extensive set of the author's own research interviews with a successful practising manager, Rebecca Rawnsley, who works in a major multinational company in the Enterprise Software sector. This material is presented separately to make clear that it is based on the experience and opinions of a particular individual. It is believed that it will prove extremely useful to the reader in helping them to recognise the reality of the application of the ideas in this book alongside a considerable amount of common sense and practical experience and that this will help them to achieve progress and positive outcomes for their organisation and themselves. In the following section of this chapter the interview series is introduced by the use of a scene-setting discussion about her background and what her work involves.

CV – REBECCA RAWNSLEY

Director, Head of Bid Management (EMEA) Company G, June 2022 to present.

Director, Head of Internal Bids & Proposals (EMEA – APAC) Company F, November 2019–May 2022

Head of Bids and Tenders, Company E Ltd, May 2016–October 2019

Senior Bid Manager, Company D, September 2013–May 2016

Bid Manager, Company C, June 2013–August 2013

Bid Manager, Company B, June 2012–June 2013

Career Break, June 2011–May 2012

Sales and Bid Coordinator, Company A Group, June 2007–June 2011

Q So you have been in a bid management role since 2012?

> Well, technically I started out back in 2007, that was in a sales and bid support role. That was how I found bidding. No one plans to go into bid management, but I joined Company A as sales admin and quickly built a good rapport with the sales director. I found out about these weird bid forms that they were continuously submitting. With that I just found my niche, my flair was for everything on which the bid management process focused, coordinating the people etc., that is where I first fell into bid management.

Q So, would I be right to say that, like most young managers, you discovered what you were good at by finding yourself there and took that up as your personal opportunity?

Yes. Career wise, I moved on a little slowly. I stayed there for four years. It was just a local small office, but it allowed me in a safe setting to get involved and test out ideas in a nice environment. Then I thought I can now move on, there is actually a bigger industry and profession for me to join in this type of role.

Q Right, OK, and so in 2012, you moved into your first bid management role as opposed to bid support?

Yes. So, then I was still an individual contributor but managing the process and coordinating the people working on the bid. I wasn't yet manager of a team, but I managed the bid itself.

Q Could you describe the group who worked on a bid?

It comes from different work streams, different areas of the business such as Finance, Marketing, Operations etc. But it was just a one-off group got together for a particular purpose. They came together with a clear core purpose; let us win the deal, put it together, build the solution, hand over to operations, and then disband. They all had other stuff they were doing as well, and it was regarded by them all as a side task.

Q OK so, could you detail what a bid manager actually does?

A bid manager provides the governance and oversight managing the internal process in response to an invitation to tender that is of interest to the company. This is especially important if it is anything that must go out to public contract, which is anything that involves taxpayers' money so requiring to be bought in a fair, transparent way. The process is always one looking for best value, not just lowest price. The bid manager consults the rules and regulations making sure that the company is compliant and is putting its best foot forward, is following due process, is not missing deadlines is pulling in additional people to the group as needed etc. Clearly the bid must read well, it must be compelling, and winnable. Really the same applies for successful private sector bidding, you need the same sort of structure. The bid manager is making sure that the bid group is working in the most efficient way, and everyone knows what they need to do and when they need to do it.

Q So would you say that if one looked, one could find a bid manager or bid managers in most major organisations?

Yes, I would say that; whether it is a formal title or whether it is some-thing individual that someone has slowly got increasingly involved in. In some cases, people are doing it without realising it.

Q OK, great. So now I have some questions about how bid management relates to other sorts of management. First, what is the relationship be-tween bid management and the general management of the organisa-tion, the senior management of the organisation?

Right, in relation to the senior management of the organisation. I, as a bid manager or head of bids or leader of the bid function, need to understand what the strategic goal is, what the central plan of the organisation is. I need to understand the go to market strat-egy, the areas of interest, what is being worked up for the future, so that I can make sure that we are finding the right opportunities and that I am helping discount those that are not right for us.

Q How does that fit then with what is often called business develop-ment? They are not the same thing are they?

The bid management lifecycle is a strand of the overall business development life cycle. For example, there can be a direct sale that never needs to touch the bid manager. Or there can be a pipeline of regular sales but at some point, this might have to go to tender be-cause of the value and then it enters the bid management lifecycle.

Q Right, if I was a business development manager in one of the com-panies that you have worked for, would you see us as working together or perhaps in parallel? Or is it that the business development manager goes off and does his or her thing and then thinks of bid management once they have generated some sort of interest or some sort of idea that a customer might want?

What should happen and what works best is that you work hand in hand with the business development manager. I see it as a tripod. We need the business development, the bid person, and the solu-tion expert. Without one of these legs, it is going to topple. All three should continuously engage with each other. It is about touching base to let everyone know an invitation to tender is coming out. Just be involved a little not holding lots of heavy meetings. Business development is certainly the opportunity owner. But it will all go wrong if they only pull in the bid person at last minute.

Q How then, does bid management relate to marketing management?

Often bid management jobs will be found listed under marketing and if bid management does not have a clearly defined function, then they will be within the marketing function. Marketing is broader. It is earlier in the overall business process. My view is that we are more a part of sales and business development because we are very closely relating to the individual customer needs. We are trying to sell this specific opportunity, this contract, rather than generating the set of opportunities in the first place.

Q Last question about other managers, how does bid management relate to operational management?

Although it is often just viewed as an admin support role and is about sales, it is not wrong to see it as a part of business operations in the broadest sense. It draws on all the different tools such as stakeholder management, change management, knowledge, and information management and so on. Bid management touches and interacts and needs input from every single area of the business. You are getting to see the whole business; it is an excellent training ground. Often the bid management process will surface lots of flaws in the current business operations processes or organisational design that you only pick up because you get to see it all the way through. Bid management is sales and operational management with added helicopter vision. I would say that bid management is the management of high value or high-volume individual customers, turning those individual customer opportunities into sales.

Q Overall then, what would you say was the impact of bid management?

I would say that key areas of impact are, firstly, business growth through new customers and the retention of existing customers with a new need. Secondly, creation and maintenance of organisational reputation through accurate and appropriate information that's presented in a strong compliant but interesting way. For example, it is important that we do not make the customer's bid evaluators waste their time reading something that does not nearly meet their needs. If we did that then they would question why we bid at all; which would be very damaging to reputation and to being taken seriously another time. Word gets around among customers in the same industry because they will talk. They will be asking each other why did they bid for this? Have you had similar bids from them? What do they do well if they can't even do a decent bid?

Q Would you say that bid management is different in different sectors or is it a generic sort of management skill?

I would say that the scope of opportunity to develop your skill differs depending on where you work. I am lucky that I started in smaller organisations, so I was able to be involved across the board and in broader business development. The skills I developed have equipped me to work in a variety of different sectors. In a large organisation, as a beginner, you would likely not be so broadly involved because they have the headcount and the resources and teams that cover everything and can spare effort to be involved in bid generation. Having said that some sectors offer more opportunity to create or sculpt a particular bid for a particular customer. But fundamentally, the skills required, and objectives of the task are generic.

MAJOR CASES FEATURED IN MANAGING IN ORGANISATIONS

Two large case studies are used to offer a helpful, albeit imaginary, context in which readers can base their thinking about the material in each of Chapters 4–9.

The case set out below, Motorsport Engineering Ltd (MEL), is used in each of Chapters 4–9 as a source of immediate worked examples of the material in each chapter. The material is applied to MEL as the penultimate part of each chapter. Readers, either individually or in class discussion, are encouraged to consider how Sarah, our imaginary manager, sets about undertaking the task of applying material from that chapter to her company.

Chapter 9, dealing with the Management of change, is followed in Chapter 10 by a full worked example of that subject based around another imaginary case, Beamingly Holiday Holdings Ltd (BHHL) the details of which may be found in Chapter 10.

Please read the MEL case here before commencing Chapter 4.

MOTORSPORT ENGINEERING LTD. (MEL) – BACKGROUND TO THE CASE

MEL is a private limited company that manufactures high performance fixing components (such as bolts, nuts, and washers) with a special focus on the motorsport, defence, and offshore oil sectors. It was established in 1990 by three engineers who were made redundant when the Jaguar brand was bought by Ford in 1989.

MEL has a hard-earned reputation, now maintained for more than 30 years, for keeping up with the latest technology in their field and for producing highest quality goods delivered on time. It has grown gradually to more than 300 employees working in administration, purchasing, marketing, design, production, and customer service departments. All are in one large building located on an industrial park in Oxfordshire near both the M4 and the M40 giving access to the wider road system in the United Kingdom. The building is not new but was refurbished soon after the company was established following early success and swift growth almost to its current size. This early success was built around their original key customer group which mainly included the Formula 1 teams located in Oxfordshire and neighbouring counties in England. This group of customers remains their most important. The founders attribute their success to their values as innovative engineers, expressed in the company mission "keeping up to date keeps us well ahead of the rest". This is reflected in well-established systems to ensure continuous improvement as part of a first-class Total Quality Management (TQM) system. An innovative approach to manufacturing systems as well as to products has allowed MEL successfully to grow, despite the highly competitive nature of all their markets by providing often urgent, on time, deliveries to their very demanding customer base.

Staff are generally rewarded near to the top of the range for the industry and staff turnover is low with many employees able to recall the early years of the business. The internal communications processes at MEL are sophisticated with a strong culture of worker participation. Management and employees are firmly linked into the broader customer network via regular customer feedback briefings.

Equally, suppliers are closely integrated into the MEL systems via regular onsite discussions. MEL and their suppliers work in a closely coordinated fashion focused on meeting the precise needs of their customers.

The original leadership team remains in charge, with the later additions of Tim Jones and Jeff Castle, although other investors have by now greatly diluted their ownership. These investors are individuals, well known to Tim Jones and Jeff Castle from within the broader automotive industry and from among the Motorsport fanbase. There is no dominant shareholder. The Management Team, each of whom owns 5% of the company shares, consists of the following.

John Smith, Managing Director

Tim Jones, Finance Director, line responsibility for Accounts and Purchasing

Joe Coles, Engineering and Production Director, line responsibility for Design, Production and Quality.

Jeff Castle, Marketing and Sales Director, line responsibility for Marketing and Customer Service.

Martin Summers, Company Secretary and Administration Director, line responsibility for Administration and Personnel.

MEL is regarded in the industry as a very well-run and successful organisation. However, recent financial performance has been giving the management team serious cause for concern. Martin Summers presented the following accounts and operational data at a meeting of the Management Team in late 2021. Pre-pandemic figures were presented to avoid drawing conclusions from the special circumstances of 2020; Martin said that he expected the final 2021 figures to be essentially the same as those for 2019. Details are given below of the resource base of MEL.

Key financial data	2019 £M	2018 £M	2017 £M
Turnover	15	19	18
Profit (Loss) Before Taxation	2.5	4.6	4.5
Net Assets (Liabilities)	6	7	7
Shareholders' Funds	5.9	6.9	6.5
Profit Margin	17%	24%	25%
Return on Company Cl Employed	41%	65%	67%

Cash flow	2019 £M	2018 £M	2017 £M
Cash In (Out) flow Operational. Activities	3.4	4.9	3.6
Taxation	−0.149	−0.7	−0.5
Company Cl Expenditure and Financial Investments		−0.2	−0.2
Equity Dividends Paid	−3.5	−3.8	−3.6
Increase (Decrease) Cash and **Equivalent**	**−0.25**	**0.2**	**−0.7**

Balance sheet	2019 £M	2018 £M	2017 £M
Land and Buildings	1.1	1.1	1.2
Plant and Vehicles	0.4	0.5	0.5
Fixed Assets	**1.5**	**1.6**	**1.7**
Stock and WIP	2.2	2.5	2.2
Trade Debtors	1.3	1.3	1.9
Bank and Deposits	1.7	1.8	1.5
Other Current Assets	0.29	0.32	0.3
Other Debtors	0.12	0.17	0.16
Prepayments	0.1	0.13	0.14
Deferred Taxation	0.068	0.015	
Current Assets	**5.8**	**6.2**	**6.2**
Trade Creditors	−0.5	−0.38	−0.38
Short Term Loans and Overdrafts	−0.028		
Bank Overdrafts	−0.028		
Corporation Tax			−0.27
Total Other Current Liabilities	−0.34	−0.15	−0.62
Current Liabilities	**−0.89**	**−0.53**	**−1.27**
Long Term Debt	−0.065		
Provisions for Other Liabilities	−0.58	=0.58	−0.40
Long Term Liabilities	**−1.23**	**−0.58**	**−0.40**
Net Assets	**5.9**	**6.9**	**6.5**

PHYSICAL RESOURCES

- Factory building on a long commercial lease with 20 years to run. The factory was fully refurbished in 1996 and subsequently well maintained as an engineering workshop.
- A variety of high-tech machining equipment, mostly purchased in the last two years. The head of Production regards this machinery as highly flexible and told Sarah that it had a life of five to ten years.
- Five branded delivery/service vehicles, leased.
- A range of IT equipment providing all the computing power needed by the company, leased.
- A variety of office and factory furnishings mostly less than 10 years old.

HUMAN RESOURCES

- 153 employees including
  - Administration and Personnel 8 (average time in employment 2 years, average age 30)
  - Purchasing 3 (average time in employment 2 years, average age 35)

- Accounts 3 (average time in employment 1.5 years, average age 27)
- Marketing 6 (average time in employment 3 years, average age 38)
- Design 10 (average time in employment 3 years, average age 35)
- Production 110 (average time in employment 10 years, average age 50, 30 members over 60)
- Quality 4 (average time in employment 15 years, average age 55, 2 members over 60)
- Customer service 4 (average time in employment 4 years, average age 40)
- Management team 5 (average time in employment 30 years, average age 61, 2 members over 70)

FINANCIAL RESOURCES

- Cash at bank £1.7M

INTELLECTUAL RESOURCES

- Trademark, the MEL brand

Jeff Castle tabled the following very worrying marketing information.
Key Market Performance Indicators

KPI	2019 (%)	2018 (%)	2017 (%)
Customer satisfaction	83	93	95
Motorsport market share	25	28	30

The Customer Satisfaction data was particularly shocking to the Management Team. They felt that they had not been aware of this area of concern at all. Jeff said that he had got these detailed data just the day before from his team, previously he had heard some rumblings, which he had mentioned to other members of the Management Team in passing, but he had not thought the problems were anything like what was revealed by the new data. He reminded the team that when they had discussed this sort of matter previously, they had always rationalised the concern away as simply representing the ups and downs of normal commercial operations and as nothing very much to worry about compared with 30 years of ongoing success.

When the others asked him to give his views about the origins of the problem, Jeff said that his team had told him that it seemed to them that the main area of customer concern was around MEL's ability quickly and effectively to design and supply bespoke fittings for their Motorsport customers. These were at the very core of the MEL business and reflected the personal interests of all the main stakeholders. John wondered aloud whether they were beginning to lose touch with the operational realities of the organisation. For themselves, Joe and Martin thought this could not be the case, MEL had always been the market leader, but they recognised, when pressed by the others, that something was amiss.

The Management Team concluded that they were right to be concerned as performance appeared to be drifting downwards. They felt that these results were not in keeping with performance expectations in their industry as a whole or that in the sectors they served or indeed their own expectations.

The Management Team also discussed the significant changes in the automotive industry amid the move to electric vehicles, a change that was already happening fast and seen to be accelerating. The challenge of this change was greater for the component makers than for the car manufacturers themselves. The latter was still making cars, but an engine manufacturer faced complete loss of their market. Jeff Castle reported that the big, internal combustion focused, component companies such as BorgWarner appeared to be opting for a strategy of acquisition to transform themselves into EV suppliers. It was reported that they planned for 5% of sales to be EV related in 2022, 25% of sales by 2025 and 45% by 2030 – just nine years away. Arguably, the situation for MEL and its direct competitors making engineered components such as fixings is not quite so dramatic, and there are also suppliers of electrical equipment to the automotive industry which may be able to accommodate to the new reality with relatively small change. But the team also noted that their Motorsport market was also under pressure, from several directions, to move in the direction of electric vehicles and a Formula E had existed now for several years.

The team concluded that the time was more than ripe for a thorough review of the strategic position. Jeff Castle was asked to supervise the project, and he appointed a member of his team, Sarah Riley, Head of CRM, to be project manager. The Management team asked for a detailed report with recommendations in three months. They needed to renew their understanding of what was happening in MEL and what their strategic options were.

Sarah's first step was to discuss the situation with the Management Team to get their perspective but also to clarify their wishes as the key shareholders in MEL. She knew that in due course, it would be necessary to get the input of other stakeholders (employees, key customers, and key suppliers), but this would follow her initial analysis of the strategic position.

She concluded that the Management Team (who have a total shareholding of 25%, making them the dominant shareholder if they stuck together) were all committed to the future success of MEL and all wished personally to be involved. They certainly were not interested, individually or collectively, in selling the business or retiring.

She also concluded that the operational position of MEL was now delicately poised between the success of the past and an uncertain future. She observed that human resources offered some causes for concern around a lack of new blood and a lack of sources of new ideas being able to be evolved or innovated in MEL. This was especially the case in Production and perhaps, she thought privately, the Management team too.

While the factory itself was well maintained, it was now of a rather dated design and layout, especially when compared with more modern workplaces. Thirdly, while financial resources still included a substantial amount of cash this would likely be reduced rapidly if current performance was not improved. The worsening customer satisfaction data likely indicated a falling offer in previous standards of service quality or that competitors had caught up and perhaps were now offering a better service than MEL.

As head of CRM, Sarah knew that the customers particularly valued the ability of MEL urgently to deliver specialist components unique to their special requirements. Talking with the Head of Production, she found that this ability was based on several key competences.

- Supplier integration
- Stock management of a wide range of certified specialised materials
- Design and machining capability always able to take on urgent tasks, often within 24 hours.
- Design and machining capability able to manufacture components to the highest quality with 100% inspection and certification.

Talking with her colleagues, Sarah concluded that the competitive advantage that MEL enjoyed, based on the ability urgently to design and machine bespoke components, was being reduced by new competitors and that this was most likely the area in which customer satisfaction was being damaged, given that supplier integration, stock management, and quality production were competences that were shared across the industry as they were required for successful operations in the sector. Currently then, there was no basis for a sustainable competitive advantage.

While Sarah was talking with the Head of Accounts, she asked also about financial performance. She was shown the following: -

- Profit Margin (Profit before Tax/Sales) has declined from 27% to 17% over the last three years.
- Return on Company Cl Employed, ROCE (Profit before Interest and Tax/Total Assets less Current Liabilities) has declined from 67% to 41% over the last three years.

Together, they concluded that this reflected the marketing data reported to the Management Team, i.e.

- Market share declining in the motorsport sector.
- Reputation, as measured by customer satisfaction, being damaged.

The detailed customer information which Sarah had in her own CRM records yielded the following information.

- Customers
  - Car racing teams
  - Motorbike racing teams
  - British Defence Manufacturing companies
  - European Defence Manufacturing companies
  - British owned North Sea Operations companies
  - US owned North Sea Operations companies
- Customer's needs
  - High performance components
  - Full material traceability
  - Quality plan management
  - Manufactured from special alloys
  - Required in a hurry
  - Bespoke to the individual customer
- How are the customer's needs being satisfied?
  - Warehousing, stock management, and certification software
  - Positive Material Identification testing equipment
  - Best-in-class design software
  - ERP manufacturing software

The external context around the MEL decline in share of the motorsport sector combined both costs pressures and the emergence of new competitors. Companies in the broader automotive components sector present a direct threat to MEL, and this was exacerbated by the mature and, to some extent, declining nature of the market in relation to traditional motor vehicles. It had long been Sarah's view and now confirmed by taking account of all this internal and external information, that the critical success factors for the future at MEL were as follows:

1. Ensure on-time response to typically urgent customer demands.
2. Offer a bespoke one-off design capability tailored to the needs of the different customers.
3. Maintain quality performance in terms of both production and delivery, tightly focused on meeting customer's precise needs.
4. Use only of certified materials.

Sarah knew from her own customer contacts and from her immediate colleagues in the marketing and sales team that MEL was no longer fully meeting customer expectations. The indications were that this revolves particularly around the first point above – the absolute need for an on-time response to customer demands. The team felt also that there might be increased opportunities among defence market customers and new customer groups were perhaps emerging as the nuclear energy industry revived. Also, wind energy was now taking centre stage in the light of energy security and other fossil fuel related concerns. In motorsport, negative attitudes to fossil fuel use were already hastening a move to EV motorsport.

Sarah felt that a good next step would be to conduct a thorough SWOT analysis with a view to clarifying for herself exactly what were the key elements of the current position of MEL.

*   Strengths

    *   Best-in-class design capability with suppliers closely integrated allowing co-creation of products to meet bespoke demands
    *   Significant cash reserves

*   Weaknesses

    *   Manufacturing wastage rates higher than industry norms
    *   Age distribution of employees in key areas likely to result in substantial early loss of skills and company knowledge.

*   Opportunities

    *   Impact of energy shortages and climate change creating opportunities in the renewables sector (wind and nuclear)
    *   Growth of electric vehicle motorsport sector

*   Threats

    *   New entrants in the motorsport components market
    *   Long term decline of traditional motorsport as the automotive sector moves to wholly electrical.

The detailed strategic analysis which Sarah then conducted resulted in the development of a strategy to rebuild the operational position of MEL. This was stated as follows.

1. *Seek to sell existing products or services into new markets, specifically EV motorsport, wind energy and nuclear energy. Conduct detailed market research in the EV motorsport, wind energy and nuclear energy markets to develop an understanding of competitors, customers, products/services, and prices.*
2. *Establish knowledge management processes to manage the decline in traditional automotive activity while retaining knowledge and key skills relevant to future markets. Also establish remedial recruitment to alleviate present concerns around staff age structure.*
3. *Take steps to stem the loss of reputation among existing key customers by improving organisational structure, organisational culture, processes, and skills to mitigate the risk that product delivered to the motorsport sector will be high priced or poorer quality than that of competitors. In the somewhat longer term these changes must lead to MEL being recognised again as the highest quality provider in all its markets.*

Sarah presented this to the management team who accepted her views. She was asked to follow up by developing an implementation plan. The details of this process are set out in Chapters 4–9.

CHAPTER SUMMARY

- The management of the people in an organisation is both difficult and crucial to success. It is by far the most difficult task facing any manager from the most junior to the most senior.
- There exist a set of practical tools which can be used by the manager to assist them in their task. These tools revolve around three key ideas.
  - Organisational behaviour – an understanding of how people and groups of people behave in an organisational setting.
  - Properties of organisations that emerge automatically from the fact of its existence such as organisational culture, power, politics, and leadership.
  - Recognition that all management is really about successfully implementing change and a kit of tools to help with this.

2 Management

THE DEVELOPMENT OF MANAGEMENT AS A CONCEPT

Management of organisations is a topic that has been written about since people first started to write. Generally, this dealt with the management of political entities and taking a look at the work of Plato,[1] Sun Tzu,[2] and Niccolo Machiavelli[3] will give a feel for the wide range of this writing and its continuing relevance to this day. However, we can regard modern understanding of management as commencing in the later days of the 19th century building on the Industrial Revolution and the understanding of the importance of specialisation and division of labour to enhance productivity, first developed in the work of Adam Smith.[4] A timeline is shown in Figure 2.1 indicating a gradual development of management thought to the modern point of view often known as Contingency Theory.

SCIENTIFIC AND ADMINISTRATIVE MANAGEMENT

In the early 20th century Frederick Winslow Taylor (1856–1915) became widely known for his methods to improve industrial efficiency.[5] These were published in his book *The Principles of Scientific Management* which dealt with a systematic study of the relationships between people and tasks for the purpose of redesigning the work process for higher efficiency. Taylor wanted to replace the rules of thumb which were then the norm in management and sought to reduce the time a worker spent on each task by optimising the way the task was done. Thus, the term

DOI: 10.4324/9781032686592-2

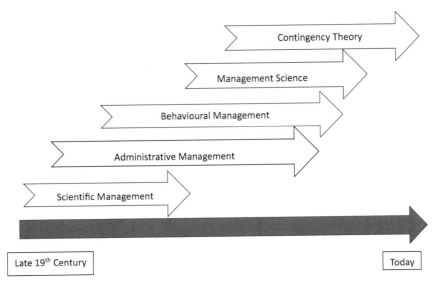

Figure 2.1 The development of modern management theory.

scientific management refers to better coordinating and organising the enterprise for everyone's benefit including providing for increased wages for workers. This approach is also often referred to as Taylor's Principles, or Taylorism. However, the reality that emerged was that managers frequently implemented only the increased output side of Taylor's plan so that workers did not share in the benefits of that increased output. Furthermore, specialised jobs became very boring, very dull, and thoroughly demotivating.

Around the same time, the German sociologist Max Weber (1864–1920) argued that bureaucracy constituted the most efficient and rational way in which human activity could be organised and that systematic processes and organised hierarchies are necessary to maintain order, to maximise efficiency, and to eliminate favouritism. The bureaucracy he described had four main elements: -

- Written rules and procedures
- A clearly specified hierarchy
- A clearly specified system of tasks and role relationships
- Systems to evaluate and reward employees fairly and equitably.

In parallel, in France, a mining engineer called Henri Fayol was developing his own administrative approach to management often called Fayolism.[6] His approach effectively includes the same ideas as offered by Taylor and Weber together; division of labour allowing for job specialisation, employees should have only one boss so that there would be unity of command and both formal and informal authority and responsibility should result from the individual's possession of special expertise. He said that the tasks of managers were to

- Ensure team performance.
- Ensure objectives achieved.
- Maintain mission and values by
  - forecasting
  - planning
  - organising
  - commanding
  - coordinating
  - controlling

This is now often expressed as *planning, organising, leading, and controlling*[7] and certainly, this does not seem a bad general statement of the task of management.

Much more recently a similar but more extensive set of managerial tasks or roles has been set out by Henry Mintzberg.[8]

- Figurehead.
- Leader.
- Liaison.
- Monitor.
- Disseminator.
- Spokesperson.
- Entrepreneur.
- Disturbance Handler.
- Resource Allocator.
- Negotiator.

My own view is that this adds little of value to the planning, organising, leading and controlling formulation based on Fayol's ideas.

BEHAVIOURAL MANAGEMENT

The behavioural approach to management is the study of how managers should behave to motivate employees and encourage them to perform at high levels and be committed to the achievement of organisational goals. Thus, it focuses on the way a manager should act personally to motivate employees. This approach originated in studies of how characteristics of the workplace affected worker fatigue and performance at the Hawthorne

Works of the Western Electric Company from 1924 to 1932. They concluded that workers responded well not to improvements in working conditions so much, but rather to being the centre of attention. More generally the behavioural (or Human Relations) approach concludes.

- The aptitudes of individuals are imperfect predictors of job performance.
- Informal organisation affects productivity.
- Work-group norms affect productivity.
- The workplace is a social system.

This is very largely, the approach adopted by the main part of this book in Chapters 3–10 given that the focus of this book is on line management, the most important and difficult element of which is the management of people.

SCIENTIFIC AND CONTINGENCY APPROACHES TO MANAGEMENT

The term "Management Science" refers to an approach to management that uses rigorous quantitative techniques to maximise the use of organisational resources. Key elements of this, which will be found operating in all substantial organisations and many smaller ones are listed below.

- **Quantitative management** – utilises linear programming, modelling, simulation systems, game theory, and chaos theory.
- **Operations management** – techniques used to analyse all aspects of the production system now including Algorithmic decision making and applications of AI.
- **Total Quality Management (TQM)** – focuses on analysing input, conversion, and output activities to increase product quality.
- **Management Information Systems (MIS)** – provide information vital for effective decision making.

It should be noted that while all of these are important, indeed essential to any organisation, this is far from a sufficient programme of activities. Quantitative techniques cannot be applied to the management of people whether they are employees or customers. Neither are these techniques more than partially capable of dealing with the immense complexity and dynamism of the external environment of the organisation (see for this the companion work to this book, Understanding Strategic Analysis[9]).

Contingency Theory is completely opposite to Management Science in its basis. It concludes that there is no one best way to organise, a calculation to find the right answer cannot in fact be done. Instead, the organisational structures and control systems that managers choose depend on, *are contingent on*, the characteristics of the external environment in which the organisation operates. Gareth Morgan[10] has summarised the main ideas underlying contingency:

- Organisations are open systems that need careful management to satisfy and balance internal needs and to adapt to environmental circumstances.
- There is not one best way of organising. The appropriate form depends on the kind of task and kind of environment one is dealing with.
- Management must be concerned, above all else, with achieving alignments and good fits between task, organisation, and environment.
- Different types of specific organisations are needed in different types of environments.

THE FUTURE OF MANAGEMENT

It would seem to be evident, writing in 2023, that the future is more uncertain and more subject to multifaceted change than at any previous point in human history; one needs to think only of climate change, the importance of Sustainable Development as set out in the UN SDGs, the end of the late 20th century Age of Plenty, shortages of key resources, the emergence of AI etc. How can organisational management respond to these immense pressures? At the very least it would seem that adaptability will be a key to survival and hence success. Would not each of these situations call for different sorts of people, organised in different ways and managed in different ways? But, is it not likely that in trying to be both efficient and flexible the organisation might end up being neither? Or is there a way of becoming what we might call an "adaptable organisation"? Does the potential for new ways of organising offered by modern ICT and AI provide a way? We have seen in recent years that the web has evolved faster than any earlier technological development and that seems to be because it is not hierarchical, it is all periphery and no centre. Is this perhaps an indication of the shape of organisational things to come?

Gary Hamel[11] has written on this subject, suggesting that looking across the centuries, social systems have proved the most adaptable of organisations and he contends that such systems should be the organisational role model for the future. An ideal management system would thus be one in which power was automatically redistributed when environmental change devalued existing managerial knowledge and competences.

This book adopts the Hamel view taking as its stance that the only management that really matters albeit it is difficult, is the task of managing people.

ISSUES IN GENERAL MANAGEMENT

This book is about line management, as stated above. It is not about the overall direction of the organisation, a topic dealt with more closely by a companion volume Understanding Strategic Analysis. However, there are several prominent issues in general management which set a very important back drop to the work of the line manager and about which it behoves all managers to be careful and alert at all times. They are each dealt with briefly in the following paragraphs.

STAKEHOLDERS

Stakeholders are those individuals or groups that depend on an organisation to fulfil their own goals and on whom, in turn, the organisation depends. Modern stakeholder theory holds that organisations have a moral obligation to all those who have a stake in the business (Freeman, 2001).[12] Managers should think of stakeholders as being divided into *internal stakeholders* (e.g., managers and employees) and *external stakeholders*, who are in one of four categories:

- *Economic* (e.g., suppliers, shareholders, banks)
- *Social/political* (e.g., government agencies)
- *Technological* (e.g., standards agencies)
- *Community* (e.g., residents, neighbouring organisations)

The manager should assess the relative power of each stakeholder over the organisation and the level of interest each takes in the activities of the organisation (see Chapter 9) and should think closely about their relationship with each stakeholder group or individual.

CORPORATE SOCIAL RESPONSIBILITY (CSR), SUSTAINABILITY, AND ETHICS

Businesses and all other organisations operate in societies and are a part of those societies. Therefore, they cannot pursue purely economic goals. Equally, social legitimacy is important to all organisations, most immediately because, if damaged this would have a potentially disastrous impact on organisational reputation and on investor, customer, and supplier relationships. Acknowledging this, Corporate Social Responsibility (CSR) is a management concept in which companies integrate social and environmental concerns in their business operations and in their interactions with their stakeholders. CSR is the way through which a company achieves a balance of economic, environmental, and social imperatives while at the same time addressing the expectations of shareholders and stakeholders.[13]

Organisations may take different attitudes to CSR. These range from a laissez-faire approach in which the view is that organisations should ensure that the law is observed, profits are made, and jobs are provided, to a so called "Shaper of Society" in which the organisation seeks actively to involve itself in positive social, environmental and market change. The crucial point here for the line manager is to be aware of their organisation's position and to ensure that they take operational decisions always which seek to deliver appropriately to that position.

Sustainable development is development that meets the needs of the present, without compromising the ability of future generations to meet their own needs.[14] It forms an important part of the more general CSR concerns above. A sustainable enterprise thus has no negative impact on the global or local environment, community, society, or economy. An organisation is described as sustainable if it matches the following criteria:

- It incorporates principles of sustainability into each of its decisions.
- It supplies environmentally friendly products or services that replaces demand for non-sustainable products and/or services.
- It is greener in its operations than the competition.
- It has made an enduring commitment to environmental principles in these business operations.

It will be evident to the reader that this will only be the case if it is equally the concern of every manager at every level in the organisation.

Ethical issues may arise both in relation to these topics and of course, more broadly around operational decision making. Ethics are a matter which must be faced at the individual level. Ethics are the responsibility of every person throughout life and this responsibility cannot be transferred to the organisation or indeed, to a more senior person. The responsibility of an individual who believes that the actions of the organisation are unethical is at the least to resign but better, to take positive action to amend the failing by effective internal action or by

'Whistleblowing' to the authorities or media about the organisation (law offers some protections to whistleblowers in many countries including the United Kingdom).

DECISION MAKING

Management is about action, the achieving of outcomes using the resources we have or can readily acquire. But before action is possible there must be decisions; about what to do, when to do it, how to do it, where to do it, and who should do it. Decision making is thus fundamental to management, and it is difficult and our abilities to do it are necessarily limited. As noted above, it is not possible to analyse and then calculate to get a correct answer in all circumstances, indeed it is very rarely the case.

Thus, rationality has limits, there are limits to cognitive ability and we are subject to cognitive biases. There are always political limits to what can be done or even what can be thought (based on position, status, and power) and there are organisational limits such as emergent outcomes, trial and error, time, budgets, and resources in general. The consequences of this are that we are always faced with four key problems in making any decision.

- Incomplete information
- Uncertain information
- Information asymmetry (hidden information)
- Moral hazard (opportunism, agency)

We should see management as a craft not a science, it is the **art** of using people and resources to achieve objectives. Success in this craft requires.

- Receptiveness to the real situation (*coup d'oeil*)
- Possession of appropriate knowledge and skills
- Having a set of appropriate behaviours
- Adoption of satisficing as the best approach in real life

Satisficing is the process of searching for and choosing an acceptable, or satisfactory response to problems and opportunities, rather than trying to make the best decision. Managers engaged in a satisficing approach explore a limited number of options and choose an acceptable decision rather than seeking, probably fruitlessly, for an optimum decision. The assumption is made that the limited options examined represent all options. The satisficing approach is designed to avoid a major problem in decision making which is never actually to decide, often known as planning paralysis, arising from all the limitations to rationality referenced above.

One of the great leaders and managers of history, Napoleon Bonaparte,[15] is alleged to have made the following comments on this important subject.

- **"Nothing is more difficult, and therefore more precious, than to be able to decide".** Decision making is the key managerial contribution to the organisation while the work is done by others, by the members of the team.
- **"Take time to deliberate, but when the time for action has arrived, stop thinking".** It is always tempting to hold off deciding to clarify this or confirm that, but most times it is a false step if the thought, the impression, has arisen already that it is time to act.
- **"In order to govern, the question is not to follow out a more or less valid theory but to build with whatever materials are at hand".** Decision making takes place in the real world not in the world as we wish it to be. The resources one has are what can be used. One must avoid analysis paralysis; in the real life condition of highly bounded rationality, satisficing rather than seeking to optimise. From this, one might conclude, by way of an ethos for managers to adopt.

- *The inevitable must be accepted.*
- *The inevitable must be turned to advantage.*
- *Value must be created from the current reality.*

ADVOCACY AND ARGUMENT – ITS ROLE IN MANAGEMENT

To advocate is publicly to support or suggest an idea, development or way of doing something. It is about persuasion, something on which all managers spend a great deal of time and energy.

Information is needed for making decisions, but how it is presented and the context in which it is presented are important influencing factors. The question to ask ourselves is what we want to persuade the audience to do and how we can do this. We must provide information that makes our case, but we must also deliver it in a way sympathetic to our audience. What we are doing here is using rhetoric, the use of language effectively to persuade, inform, educate, or entertain.

The starting point is correctly to identify the rhetorical situation, which is correctly to detail and understand the circumstances in which we are seeking to communicate. Several points are key to understanding this.

- You and your relationship with the audience, the degree of credibility which you bring to the task.
- Purpose, your expected end point for this occasion and acceptable fallback points should things not go too well.
- Audience, their existing knowledge and beliefs about the topic, an assessment of their likely current response to your suggestions.
- Context, the broader situation around your proposal such as its urgency and related risks.

Success, following on from this assessment, will depend on being seen as relevant and being easy to understand and digest. Your presentation, in whatever form, must be impactful, both visually and intellectually. Key points must be signposted and highlighted. It is necessary always to involve the audience, building a good rapport. This rapport is fundamental, the creation of a congenial atmosphere, the objective being to make it more likely that the audience will understand, become sympathetic and respond positively. The details of what must be done to build rapport depend crucially on the context and relationship with the audience but, in general, presentational guidelines are as follows.

- Vocabulary – use short words that mean something to the audience.
- Sentence structure – use short sentences, active and imperative verbs.
- Logical structure – ensuring completeness, considering and addressing possible objections before they are made by the audience.
- Style – carefully judge the appropriate level of formality, showing respect for your audience.
- Body language – use open, inclusive gestures.
- Presentation structure – say what you are going to say, say it, then say what you said – in six steps.

  1. **Introduction** – purpose, say what you are going to conclude.
  2. **Position** – brief outline of the current situation and consequences.
  3. **Problem** – the audience's need that can be met by agreeing with your proposal.
  4. **Possibilities** – main alternatives approaches.
  5. **Proposal** – recommendation, supporting evidence.
  6. **Postscript** – summary of what you said, then setting out the next step.

Of course, the situation you face may be the opposite, it may be that proposals are being made with which you do not agree and wish successfully to oppose. This is the process of rebuttal.

Here are a few things to remember about rebuttal.

- Firstly, simply to say that the other side is wrong is never enough.
- Pick the important points – try to rebut the most important points of the other side's case.
- Apply logic – e.g. that the position is self-contradictory (or leads to a contradiction; a *reductio ad absurdum*) or that the conclusion does not follow from the premises (i.e. there are *non-sequiturs*) or that coincidental occurrences are being linked as if there was cause and effect (the *post hoc* fallacy).
- Identify the negative impact on third parties that accepting the argument would have (an argument based on *Pathos*).
- Play the ball, not the man – never criticise the speaker (*the ad hominem fallacy or argument based on ethos*), rather criticise what is being said.

TOOLS OF THE MANAGER

As remarked above under the discussion of decision making, management as practiced is a craft. That is, it is an activity involving skill in making things. Good managers are people who have the capability to make something well by application of their personal skill and experience. Both must be acquired, and an apprenticeship is the best approach. Academic learning alone is very inadequate to the purpose.

There are tools of the trade, and it is necessary to learn to use them well. There are rules of thumb, but there is no scientific theory, and certainly, there are no axioms. Rather, there exist many models, the most important of which are set out in subsequent chapters, but these models are very simplistic and in no way approach a complete description of the organisational situations to which they are applied.

Having said that nothing about management itself is new. There are new technologies and new descriptive and predictive models are developed from time to time but in the end, management is simply the art of using people and resources to achieve objectives. Most everything we need to know on this topic was discovered already in the depths of past time. The managed and the managers have not changed behaviourally in uncounted millennia. There is no need to reinvent the fundamentals of the management wheel.

In the spirit of learning from the past and from other complex, dynamic, and dangerous situations we might ask what is the learning on this to be found in the thousands of years of military history? General Clausewitz wrote, in his famous book "On War",[16]

> When all is said and done, it really is the commander's *coup d'œil*, his ability to see things simply, to identify the whole business of war completely with himself, that is the essence of good generalship. Only if the mind works in this comprehensive fashion can it achieve the freedom it needs to dominate events and not be dominated by them.

Box 2.1   Adapted from Wikipedia Accessed on 9 January 2024

Carl Philipp Gottfried (or **Gottlieb**) **von Clausewitz** (1 June 1780 to 16 November 1831) was a Prussian general and military theorist who stressed the psychological and political aspects of waging war. His most notable work, *Vom Kriege* ("*On War*"), though unfinished at his death, is considered a seminal treatise on military strategy and science.

Clausewitz was a realist who drew heavily on the rationalist ideas of the European Enlightenment. He stressed the dialectical interaction of diverse factors, noting how unexpected developments unfolding under the "fog of war" (i.e., in the face of incomplete, dubious, and often erroneous information and great fear, doubt, and excitement) call for rapid decisions by alert commanders. He argued that war could not be quantified or reduced to mapwork, geometry, and graphs.

REBECCA RAWNSLEY – A MODERN MANAGEMENT CAREER

Q what would you say were the key skills and the most important day-to-day activities in your own role and from your experience as a manager generally?

> I think one of the important skills is to build a level of credibility, this is maybe my personal perspective but that is how I try to behave, I like also to know that the whole team understand what I am doing and why. I feel it is important to ensure that they have a broad understanding, an overview level of understanding of the value that that team is bringing and what the team's activities should look like. This

is so much better than the usual situation you come across in which teams feel that they are just another undistinguished part of another big organisation. It is just about, as a manager, being genuine and transparent, having a general awareness and being honest and truthful I think that is key. It is certainly not about interfering in everyone's day to day work! All the team members are grown-ups, we can speak, we do not need to hold anything back, we need to share what we are doing together. Some people might describe it as walking the job, certainly it includes being readily available, offering support as required.

Q OK. I think we can see that as a, as a skill, an attitude to the people you work with and an attitude to your own work. Now, would you say that was different from a leadership role?

I think there's an important difference between managing and leading. Yes, I think managing effectively is crucial and it is task oriented, often it may be reactive although ideally not. I think managing is generally to do with the day-to-day and I think leading is about future vision and figuring out the path to get somewhere and how successfully to take everyone along on that journey. I think. a leader can be taught to manage but I do not think a manager can necessarily be taught to lead. Leaders must have the tricky conversations and engage with everyone and line people up for the future and this will certainly involve change. We could characterise leadership as being about transformation and management as about transaction. So, in talking about management, we are talking about day-to-day activities and the transaction of those day-to-day activities in the best way. It is about creating a framework for the work to be done and providing the necessary resources. The framework is around people, processes, tools, and reporting. Based on the reporting, feedback, we can do some continuous improvement, we can refine and get better. The manager needs to put all this in place and then the only interference in the work itself is by exception. If the people in the team know that you trust them, they will come to you to ask you to step in when they need it. During the operation of the framework the normal role of the manager is to keep it in good shape, keep improving it and praise the efforts of the team.

Q So, is that about motivation?

Yes, that's what you need to be able to do, and I think that's what is really key is to equip the people in your team with the necessary skills and resources. Equip them with the tools so they can stay calm, do the work and make the necessary decisions although that ability is what is often lacking. You need people that can make decisions, you cannot possibly make them all yourself any more than you can have all the skills and all the knowledge, and all the contacts encompassed by your whole team. To make decisions, of course, they need to be motivated to make decisions rather than taking the easy option of passing the question on. Of course, they need to have the specific decision-making skills and experience that are required in the particular circumstances, but you must also remove the fear, because that's often a driver for non-decision making. The team must know they are trusted and will be backed.

CHAPTER SUMMARY

This chapter identifies that.

- Current thinking on management adopts a contingency approach, there are no right answers, and it is not possible to seek to achieve a completely correct management action.
- It is contended that the organisation as a social system is the right way to think about organisations going forward.
- Issues in general management that are the responsibility of all managers, who should ensure therefore their personal awareness of these topics, are the power and interests of their stakeholders, Corporate Social Responsibility stance and ethical operations.
- Important skills to be developed by all managers are decision making and advocacy.

NOTES

1 Plato. (2007) *The Republic*, London: Penguin Random House.
2 Sun, T. (1994) *The Art of War*, Hachette: Basic Books.
3 Machiavelli, N. (2014) *The Prince*, London: Penguin Random House.
4 Smith, A. (1977) *An Inquiry into the Nature and Causes of the Wealth of Nations*, Chicago, IL: University of Chicago Press.
5 Taylor, F.W. (2006) *The Principles of Scientific Management*, New York: Cosimo Classics.
6 Fayol, H. (1949) *General and Industrial Management*, Bath: Pitman & Sons.
7 Daft, R.L. (1983) *Organization Theory and Design*, Eagan, MN: West Publishing Company.
8 Mintzberg, H. (1973) *The Nature of Managerial Work*, New York: Harper & Row.

 9 Elsworth, T. (2023) *Understanding Strategic Analysis*, London: Routledge.
10 Morgan, G. (2006) *Images of Organisations*, London: Sage.
11 Hamel, G. (2007) *The Future of Management*, Brighton, MA: Harvard Business School.
12 Freeman, E. and McVea, J. (2001) A Stakeholder approach to strategic management. In M. Hitt, E. Freeman, and J. Harrison (Eds.), *Handbook of Strategic Management*. Oxford: Blackwell Publishing.
13 UNIDO, https://www.unido.org/, accessed 4th December 2023.
14 UN, Report of the Brundtland Commission, https://www.un.org/, accessed 4th December 2023.
15 Chandler, D. (2002) *The Military Maxims of Napoleon*, Newbury: Greenhill Books.
16 von Clausewitz, C. (1984) [1832]. M. Howard and P. Paret (Eds.), *On War* [*Vom Krieg*] (Indexed ed.). Princeton, NJ: Princeton University Press.

3 Organisational Behaviour, Leadership, and Management of Change in Perspective

WHAT IS AN ORGANISATION?

Following Buchanan and Huczynski[1] we say that an organisation is a social arrangement for achieving controlled performance in pursuit of collective goals.

- Organisations are made up of groups of people who interact with each other. The size of these groups varies from two to very many and, typically, the groups are themselves grouped into higher level groups until, eventually the whole organisation is encompassed. But it is important to note that there will usually be many other outside groups, belonging to other organisations, which make key contributions in the guise, e.g., of supplier or partner.
- Membership of the organisation implies shared objectives and the fundamental driver here is to achieve goals which would be beyond the reach of the individual alone. Organisations are concerned with controlled performance in the pursuit of these goals, and it is this performance which determines the success and ultimate survival of the organisation. But it is important to note here that organisations tend to develop a life of their own as a purely social entity the members of which; because of the social values that accrue, will always seek to enable its survival even when it is weak in performing towards its goals.

Given that all resources are limited, most notably this applies to time which can never be replaced, performance has to be both efficient and effective and the need for this leads to a deliberate and ordered allocation of functions, or division of labour, between an organisation's

DOI: 10.4324/9781032686592-3

members. It may be said therefore that organisations exist for a variety of practical reasons such as to provide.

- Increases specialisation and division of labour.
- Enable use of large-scale technology.
- Manage the external macro and competitive environments.
- Reduce transaction costs.
- Exert power and control over suborganisations and individuals.
- Etc.

UNDERSTANDING ORGANISATIONAL BEHAVIOUR

Organisational Behaviour, a term first coined in the 1950s but built on academic work done in the 1920s, 1930s and 1940s, is behavioural in its approach and is defined as "the study of the structure and management of organisations, their environments, and the actions and interactions of their individual members and groups".

But organisations have not always been seen in quite in this way. Preceding the academic work just mentioned the general view taken of organisations was based on the ideas of economists, it was the so-called Classical View of Organisations. This held that they are rational entities, scientifically designed to deliver the outcomes intended. Furthermore, the Classical View held that organisations are populated by people motivated solely by money with a mindset of maximising reward and minimising effort. Consequently, it was thought that jobs had to be designed to maximise management control and minimise individual discretion. This rationalist approach to management is often known as Taylorism.

There is now an alternative view, developing as noted in the paragraph above in the mid part of the 20th century, which we might call the "Human Relations" view of organisations. The key elements of this are a recognition that people are emotional rather than economic-rational beings and that organisations are cooperative, social systems rather than mechanical constructs. In fact, it is said, organisations are composed of informal structures, rules, and norms as well as explicitly stated formal practices and procedures. This is, partly, the view adopted in this book, and which is based ultimately, on the practical, day to day, experience of managers in all types of organisations going back millennia. In this book, we adopt the view that management is solely about people, and we note that, behaviourally, people have not changed at all from people in the past albeit we all now work amongst technology and undertake tasks that are very different from the technology and tasks of even just a few years ago. Accordingly, the real management practice of the past, rather than any theoretical position, is a most excellent guide to how to manage.

However, it is important also to recognise that all organisations, like all communities, especially in the modern word, are connected, sometimes closely, sometimes distantly, to all other organisations. In other words, organisations are open systems interacting with their external environment. This implies that the best organisational structure and the best approach to undertaking whatever are the organisation's activities is dependent upon the circumstances, the situational variables, faced by it. We conclude that there is no best or correct way to design and operate an organisation, simply that there is the best way we can come up with for the present. This has been called the "Contingency" view of organisations.

Thus, in summary, the main idea underlying this book is that organisations, of whatever type, are simply social entities and that the study of them forms part of a wider field known as Organisational Theory, that is the sociological study of the structures and operations formal social organisations. Helms[2] in his Encyclopaedia of Management describes this area of theory as having origins and contributions from sociology, anthropology, philosophy, and political science. Organisation theory as a topic for managers, as opposed to scholars, has emerged recently. There has of course, been interest in organisation in terms of how groups arrange social systems and status systems as long as the human condition has been studied. Certainly, it is true that the organisations we discuss in this book have special purposes such as the production and sale of a product or service but then this is also the case for many of the things we normally think of as societies, such as the village football club. We should expect therefore that whatever we know to be true about human society in general will apply also to the organisation in which we work as a manager. This may seem obvious and indeed the reality is that working managers, always, have understood this to be the case when it comes to the practical performance of their task.

The above is one sense in which all organisations are alike and maybe understood to behave, in similar ways. There are also other senses in which this same realisation is true, that all organisations are alike.

- Firstly, all organisations exist to divide up large and complex tasks and to co-ordinate the separate outcomes i.e. they exist to *differentiate* and *integrate*.
- Secondly, as we have noted already, all organisations have a purpose and an identity; but subject to some variation by their

economic role or sector, they share also a fundamental operational logic:

- Commercial organisations in the private sector, are based on a logic of profit and return on investment.
- In the public sector, the logic is accountability for the use of public funds and
- In the third sector or social economy, we might say that there is a logic of commitment to a cause.

Equally, there are some things which tend to make organisations all very different from each other:

- Firstly, the size of an organisation has a big impact on how it operates and what it feels like to work in.
- Secondly, the particular technology and physical location of an organisation have a big impact on how it operates and what it feels like to work in.
- Thirdly, all organisations exhibit a life cycle operating and feeling different in terms of organisational culture at each stage. Daft (1994) suggests there are four stages:
  - *Birth* – entrepreneurial in character, founders show a strong sense of ownership, integration of the organisation is by force of personality.
  - *Youth* – some delegation of authority is now needed, division of labour begins to emerge, operating systems start to be formalised.
  - *Midlife* – fully formalised, problems of poor integration are now exhibited, and a loss of flexibility and loss of creativity start to emerge.
  - *Maturity* – now set in its ways, ponderous decision making is the norm, there is a danger of stagnation, the organisation is now wide open to competitive threat.[3]

Clearly, the management function itself is also a source of similarity and variability between organisations. All managers are subject to a fundamental set of external and internal environmental variables, but they are variables which are context dependant. Deresky[4] has suggested a useful diagram bringing together the complete set of variables (Figure 3.1).

This book is, however, a practical guide to managing in organisations so we will not dwell further on these very broad and fundamental considerations. Rather, in the sections below, there is an outline of the theoretical background to each of the fields of knowledge around organisational behaviour that will be found directly to benefit the practical manager.

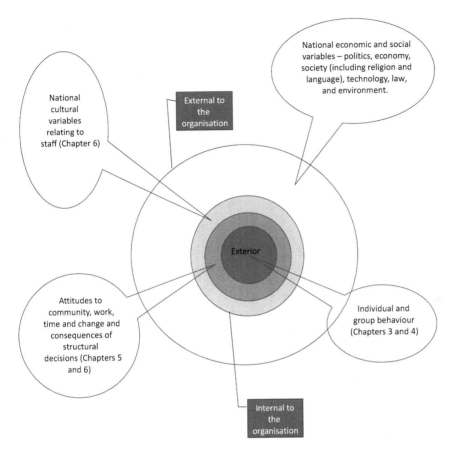

Figure 3.1 Variables affecting managers.

INDIVIDUAL BEHAVIOUR IN ORGANISATIONS, SEE CHAPTER 4

What can we expect about the behaviour of individuals in an organisational context? It is a difficult question; we should recognise that every individual is different from every other to some degree and we have noted above that all organisations are different to some degree. Combining these two sets of differences makes for a very wide range of answers to our question. On the other hand, as seen above, it is also true that organisations are often quite alike, and we may often see strong similarities in the ways in which individuals behave given similar circumstances. We can perhaps expect to be somewhat able to predict behaviour if we know enough about the circumstances and we understand how these are perceived and how they influence the attitudes and responses of people in general.

Fundamentally this is the study of motivation; what is it that persuades people to act in a given way in given circumstances? What is it that leads people to work well and hard, to persist and overcome obstacles, to be enthusiastic about their work and do more than the minimum? It should be noted that this topic refers to the average person not to any individual each of whom we would need to know very well in order reliably to predict their behaviour. Motivation is a complex topic and there are several well-known theoretical approaches to understanding motivation including: -

- Maslow's theory of Human Motivation and Needs
- Herzberg's Two Factor theory of Motivation
- Expectancy theory
- Equity theory
- The Job Characteristics model

There is a good deal of common sense in all these approaches but there also some implications of theory that do not necessarily accord with the everyday view of what people will find motivating. As this is a practical guide to managing, we focus in Chapter 4 on the most well known and most commonly discussed theories and then in particular on the theoretical approaches (Herzberg and Expectancy Theory) most likely to give benefit day to day. It will be observed that these are also the theories of motivation most widely known amongst practising managers.

GROUP AND TEAM BEHAVIOUR, SEE CHAPTER 5

Of course, it is the case that organisations consist of individuals, perhaps just a few or perhaps very many. But they do not usually work solely as individuals. They work in various suborganisations, often called groups or teams. These are then assembled into bigger suborganisations with names such as department or division (see Chapter 6). The question to be addressed in this chapter is to ask what we can expect of the collective behaviour of these groups. There is of course the question asked previously about the motivation of each individual but now the individuals and their motivation interact with each other to form an overall behaviour of the group.

We will look at the key factors impacting how groups behave including size of the group, nature of the task to be undertaken, the resources and support possessed by the group, the degree of external recognition enjoyed by the group and the composition of the group with particular attention to the questions of diversity and inclusion. This will lead us to an understanding of how group behaviour can be improved and of the ways in which it can fall short of expectations.

The meaning of the term "team" is the same in organisations as in general usage although in organisations the word is often abused to describe what is really just a collection of employees. A team properly so called is a special group in which members have joint objectives, are in regular contact, share responsibility and support each other and are co-ordinated by a team leader. We will look at how this special sort of group develops from the more general form. A key set of ideas here is Tuckman and Jensen's model of Team Formation indicating that a group needs to go through a set of steps known as Forming, Storming, Norming and Performing[5] before they can become a high-performing team. We will look also at how the behaviour of a team may depend on both individual and group behavioural factors.

ORGANISATIONAL DESIGN, SEE CHAPTER 6

This chapter deals with how the building blocks of the organisation, the groups and teams referred to above, are brought together in a series of complex structures designed to enable delivery of the organisational objectives (hence, there is a strong link here with strategic decision making). There are two steps in this: firstly, the question of structure and then secondly, that of design to achieve a specific set of objectives.

Structuring of the organisation deals with decisions about co-ordination and control. The former involves the management of internal information flows to facilitate decision making whereas control involves the distribution of decision-making rights and authority within the organisation. There are decisions to be made about the degree of centralisation or decentralisation of authority within the organisation including whether this should vary across different parts of the organisation. In general, these are all features which are not evident to the outside observer.

Organisational design deals with the overall shape of the organisation and is often to be found published in the form of organisation charts. There are many and often very complex organisation structures in use by organisations large and small. However, they have been categorised into three main types, the unitary structure, the divisional structure, and the matrix structure:

- The first of these collects all the people working in each type of activity or function, into a specialist suborganisation under the leadership of a senior practitioner of that function. It is sometimes called a Functional structure.

- The Divisional structure collects all the people working on a particular project or product or service or in a particular location into a suborganisation headed by a senior practitioner from that field of endeavour.
- The matrix structure is a mixture in which people report both to a senior functional leader and a senior project, product, service, or location leader.

Most major organisations have some sort of complex variation on all three of these simultaneously.

In this context it is worth noting the advice of Peter Drucker[6]

> Good organisation structure does not by itself produce good performance. But poor organisation structure makes good performance impossible, no matter how good the individuals.

ORGANISATIONAL CULTURE, POWER, AND POLITICS, SEE CHAPTER 7

In this book we argue that organisations are human societies and therefore, will exhibit all the characteristics of society in general. Once an organisation has been created it is to be expected that, over time, the normal aspects that we will observe in any society will emerge. Specifically, we will see organisational culture, the use and abuse of Organisational Power and the Political Behaviour used to acquire and deploy power within the organisation. The successful manager will be able to navigate these complex areas of organisational life in such a way as to optimise the performance of the organisation and achievement of its objectives.

Organisational Culture might be thought of as the personality of an organisation. It decides how things are done in an organisation daily. It affects how employees perform their work; how they relate to each other; to their customers and to their managers. Organisational culture affects not only task issues – how well or badly an organisation performs, but also emotional issues – how workers feel about their work and their organisation. Ann Cunliffe[7] states that organisational culture is important because it shapes the image that the public has of an organisation, it influences organisational effectiveness, it provides direction for the company and helps to attract, retain and motivate staff.

Organisational Power and Politics are intimately connected topics. Buchanan and Huczynski[8] have defined them in this way "those activities undertaken within an organisation to acquire, develop and use power and other resources to obtain one's preferred outcomes in a situation in which there is uncertainty or an absence of consensus about choices". It will be seen that the effective manager will need to be aware of the potential sources of power within the organisation and to develop the skills and relationships to be able to acquire and use that power. This will be particularly important at times of change and doubt about organisational direction.

LEADERSHIP, SEE CHAPTER 8

Leadership is also a natural consequence of the existence of a society, indeed in any group however small leadership will emerge. This topic deserves a chapter of its own as arguably the single most important factor in organisational success. Northouse[9] describes leadership as the process whereby an individual influences a group of individuals to achieve a common goal. Leadership is a topic that has been written about since earliest times. The search for leadership and the giving and acceptance of leadership are fundamental parts of the human condition. Many great leaders have written of their own approach and there is much of value to be learned from reading their views. My own favourite, allegedly due to Napoleon Bonaparte, is that leaders are "dealers in hope".

In this chapter we shall seek to dispel several key myths about leadership such as.

- That leadership outcomes are attributable wholly to the leader, the hero, the "Great Man" – whereas, in fact the real agency of leadership is through the actions of the leader's followers.
- That there is a formula for effective leadership – but in fact leadership is highly dynamic and must be approached in the light of the current situation.
- That the results of leadership are more important than the processes by which they are achieved that is that the ends justify the means – but the social role of the leader, what they symbolise, how effectively they motivate, what they represent to followers about the future and the ethical situation, are all crucial.

Our favoured approach is to recognise that leadership is a dynamic system which occurs in society. That is that leadership is always contingent and is based on an interlocking set of factors which are:

- The context
- The leader's recognition of the context and relationship with the followers

- The follower's motivation and ability to deliver organisational outcomes given the context

MANAGEMENT OF CHANGE, SEE CHAPTER 9

Change is a fundamental part of the experience of the line manager. The external environment of the organisation is subject to continuous change driven by forces large and small, these are both distant in origin such as legal and political change and nearby among customers, competitors, and suppliers. Equally the organisation itself is in a state of continuous change as resources, products and services of all types pass through their life cycle. The people in the organisation of course themselves change through all the natural processes of everyday life.

It will be seen that all this change happening continuously and simultaneously will produce a very complex set of challenges and opportunities for the organisation and hence for the line manager as the change impacts the operations of the organisation. Responding to these drivers of change will require significant investment, a significant amount of time and, most particularly, will cause the daily lives and short, medium, and long-term activities and career prospects of employees to change.

It will be seen that responding to this ferment is likely to be very difficult and fraught with the risk of unexpected outcomes and unfulfilled hopes and plans. Even when everything goes well the world outside the organisation does not stand still to wait for past changes to be completed. It moves on, perhaps in unexpected directions and at an unanticipated speed.

There is an area of management expertise that focuses in this area called the Management of Change. Key tools of the change manager, discussed in Chapter 8, include:

- Stakeholder Management,[10] understanding the points of view and influence of all our stakeholders.
- Lewin's Force Field Analysis[11] identifying and evaluating the forces in favour of the change in hand and those opposed.
- Lewin's 3 Phase Model,[12] used as a structure for managing the change process.
- Change Agency, the identification and deployment of people to help successfully to implement the change.

CHAPTER SUMMARY

This chapter sets out the overall theoretical background to the development of understanding of the field of line management i.e., the management of organisations to deliver whatever mission they were set up to achieve. It offers a brief introduction to the material covered extensively in each of the subsequent chapters. If it is wished to use this book as a resource rather than to study the subject end to end than these sections will provide a sort of content index. The references to this chapter will be found to offer the reader a substantial library of relevant source material the study of which can lead to formation a detailed theoretical understanding of line management.

NOTES

1 Buchanan, D.A. and Huczynski, A.A. (2019) *Organizational Behaviour* (10th Ed.), Harlow: Pearson.
2 Helms, M.M. (2021) *Encyclopedia of Management*, Dundee: Thomson.
3 Daft, R.L. (1993) *Managerial Decision Making Management* (3rd Ed.), Orlando, FL: The Dryden Press.
4 Deresky, H. (2011) *International Management: Managing across Borders and Cultures*, Hoboken, NJ: Prentice Hall.
5 Tuckman, B.W. and Jensen, M.A.C. (1977) Stages of small-group development revisited. *Group & Organization Studies*, 2(4): 419–427.
6 Drucker, P. (2007) *The Essential Drucker*, London: Routledge.
7 Cunliffe, A.L. (2008) *Organisational Theory*, London: Sage.
8 Buchanan, D.A. and Huczynski, A.A. (2019) *Organizational Behaviour* (10th Ed.), Harlow: Pearson.
9 Northouse, P.G. (2019) *Leadership Theory and Practice*, London: Sage.
10 Hayes, J. (2018) *The Theory and Practice of Change Management* (5th Ed.), Basingstoke: Palgrave MacMillan.
11 Lewin, K. (1947) *Field Theory in Social Science*, New York: Harper & Row.
12 Lewin, K. (1947) *Field Theory in Social Science*, New York: Harper & Row.

4 Understanding Individual Behaviour

INTRODUCTION

In Chapter 2, we noted that it is potentially a complex matter to predict the behaviour of individuals in an organisational context. Individuals are different from each other. Organisations also are different from each other and so are the situations in which organisations and their people find themselves. However, it is also true that organisations are often quite alike, and this is somewhat true of people too. So, if we know enough about the situation and how people see the situation then we may well be able to understand what the responses of people might be. Here then we are talking about what it is that motivates people to act in a particular way in given circumstances.

In an organisational management context, it will be very important to develop this understanding and to be able to understand when people will work well and work hard, when they will persist and when they will struggle to overcome obstacles. In other words when will people willingly do more than the minimum required by the demands of contract or discipline or social pressure?

The most well-known theoretical approaches to understanding motivation include the following.

- Maslow's theory of human motivation and needs (often known as his Hierarchy of Needs)
- Herzberg's two factor theory of motivation
- Expectancy theory
- Equity theory
- The job characteristics model

DOI: 10.4324/9781032686592-4

The study of motivation is fascinating and likely to be very reward-
ing to the manager and leader, so we offer below an outline of each
of these theories. But this book is a practical guide to managing, so we
focus in this on the most well known and most widely discussed theories. This is because managers in general are aware of and use regularly
the terminology involved, even though they may not all have a full understanding of the theoretical background. Then we focus further on
those theoretical approaches (Herzberg and Expectancy Theory) that
I have found to be most likely to give benefit to the manager day to day.
In other words, we look most closely at theory that will not only yield
understanding but will offer practical tools to enable the manager to
do something positive and effective based on their understanding.

MASLOW'S THEORY OF HUMAN MOTIVATION AND NEEDS

Abraham Maslow (1908–1970) studied psychology and developed a
step-by-step theory of causes and motivations of human behaviour commonly known as Maslow's Hierarchy of Needs.[1]

Maslow classified human needs under nine headings but in modern
management discussion these are usually simplified to five, listed from
highest to lowest, the needs for:

Self-actualisation: the desire for personal fulfilment, to
develop one's potential, to become everything that one
can become.
Esteem: need for strength, confidence, achievement,
self-esteem, independence, and for reputation, prestige,
recognition, attention and appreciation, and the respect
of others.
Social interaction: need for attachment, belongingness,
affection, love, relationships.
Safety: need for security, comfort, tranquillity, freedom from
fear and threat from the environment, for shelter, order,
predictability, an organised world.
Physiological requirements: need for sunlight, sexual
expression, food, water, rest, and oxygen – needs basic
for our survival.

Maslow says that at any given time in a person's life all five needs are
present, but only one is dominant. Further, needs higher up the list usually do not become good motivators until those lower down have been
largely satisfied and that once needs are satisfied they no longer act

as a motivator. Having said that, it is acknowledged that experience of self-actualisation stimulates desire for more. Self-actualisation cannot be satisfied in the same way as the other needs.

Maslow argued that we have an innate desire to work our way up the list, pursuing the satisfaction of our higher order needs once our lower order needs are satisfied. The other side of the coin is that a lack of need satisfaction can cause frustration, anxiety, and depression due to lack of self-esteem, loss of the respect of others, an inability to sustain relationships, and an inability to develop one's capabilities.

Taken together, this suggests that the role of management so far as motivation goes, is to enable individuals to find meaning in their work, i.e., self-actualisation and to provide the opportunity to develop as far as they are able so that motivation is maintained. But not all jobs, perhaps quite a few jobs or even most jobs, may not be capable of supporting the self-actualisation of the employee. How practical then is this approach to understanding motivation? How should the manager assess the needs and need situation of their people? How should managers act to build motivation? None of this seems very clear; Maslow's approach is perhaps foundational but does not seem to help managers to act, which is, after all, what managers must do.

EQUITY THEORY

The equity theory approach to motivation is based on our reaction to our perceptions of unfair treatment. Stacy Adams (1963)[2] argued that we are motivated to act in situations which we perceive to be inequitable or unfair whether this is in our personal favour or not. Equity theory argues that the more intense the perceived inequity the stronger the motivation to act. Underreward is seen as unfair and we will act somehow to correct this unfairness. Over reward, if it is substantial, causes us to feel guilty so we will act to correct this too.

This would seem to accord with our everyday understanding of how people feel and there is research evidence giving these ideas direct support.[3] There are certainly implications for management practice, given that all employees compare their pay with that of their colleagues. It is important therefore to recognise that perceptions of inequity can create large-scale resentment in an organisation. This means that circulation of accurate information about rewards can be a really important step for management to take.

However, more generally, if one wishes to use this theory as a basis for addressing levels of motivation in the workplace, there are real difficulties. Firstly, the theory depends on individual subjective perceptions and opinions so that different people may well arrive at entirely different conclusions as to the degree of unfairness and as to the propriety of any response. Secondly, it is also not obvious in any specific organisational context whether people will make comparisons with immediate colleagues, or with people across the whole organisation or perhaps in other organisations, other sectors, etc. All of this makes equity theory fall into the category of interesting and theoretically sound but not very practical, alongside Maslow's Hierarchy of Needs.

HERZBERG'S TWO FACTOR THEORY OF MOTIVATION

Herzberg's approach is known widely as the Two Factor Theory of motivation. From interviewing large numbers of engineers and accountants Herzberg (1959)[4] concluded that dissatisfaction came from background factors such as poor pay, lack of job security, bad working relationships with colleagues and supervisors, poor working conditions, and insufficient status. He described these as hygiene factors. Hygiene factors are not, however, motivators but are the prerequisites for motivation. Similarly, he concluded that satisfaction came from the job itself with factors such as achievement, recognition, responsibility, advancement, growth which he described as motivation factors. Thus, Motivators relate to job content and hygiene factors relate to job context.

Motivator factors: aspects of work which can lead to high levels of satisfaction, motivation and performance, including:

- Achievement,
- Recognition,
- Responsibility,
- Advancement,
- Growth,
- Work itself.

Hygiene factors: aspects of work which if good, can remove dissatisfaction, but do not contribute to motivation and performance, including:

- Pay,
- Company policy,
- Supervision,
- Status,
- Security,
- Physical working conditions.

The main point here is to recognise that the opposite of being dissatisfied and hence demotivated is not to be satisfied and so motivated, but rather it is to be not dissatisfied. This does not in itself lead to being motivated. Equally, being dissatisfied reduces or negates the opportunity to be motivated. Both hygiene factors and motivation factors are important, together, to the creation of a motivated workforce and thus always need management attention.

This work by Herzberg was done quite a long while ago now but there is relatively recent research[5] suggesting that it remains relevant. Improvement in the hygiene or context factors will remove dissatisfaction but will not increase motivation and performance. The design of jobs to increase motivation and performance and the day-to-day management to maintain motivation, must focus on motivation factors, e.g., by removing controls, increasing responsibilities and accountability, and by providing feedback. Money, on the other hand, is not an overriding concern for most people, and 'bribing' people to perform better with cash incentives can be seen as manipulative and controlling. Incentive payment schemes also discourage risk-taking and creativity and undermine interest in the job itself. Pay can sometimes buy compliance, but certainly, it does not encourage commitment.

Here then we can see that Herzberg's ideas are a practical approach to managing motivation since, using the idea of motivator and hygiene factors, managers can figure out what to do to improve the motivational situation of their people and, broadly, these are factors within the control of managers (Figure 4.1).

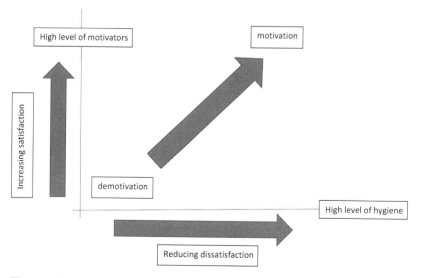

Figure 4.1 A visualisation of the operation of Herzberg's two factor theory of motivation.

EXPECTANCY THEORY

Maslow and Herzberg assume that people are motivated by rewards or incentives enabling them to meet their needs. But there is no guarantee that rewards will lead to continuing increases in effort (e.g., a promotion may quite likely have only a temporary effect on effort or may have no impact at all). Nor is there a guarantee that more effort will lead to improved performance (e.g., because skills or resources are inadequate). It might be thought that what is required is that improved performance is known or, at least, believed to increase the likelihood of reward and that improved performance will follow from enhanced effort.

Vroom (1964)[6] developed the expectancy theory of work motivation, taking these ideas forward. Expectancy theory argues that individual motivation depends on the value of outcomes, the expectation that effort will lead to good performance, and the likelihood of performance producing valued outcomes. This is all perhaps best understood diagrammatically, as set out in Figure 4.2; effort exerted will lead to good performance if the job circumstances, the resources provided, and the abilities of the individual are all appropriate. This effort will then be rewarded, and this reward is assessed by the worker as to whether it feels fair. If it does then effort will be exerted again, at least to the same

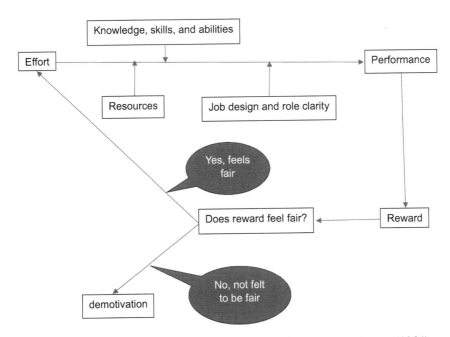

Figure 4.2 A visualisation of expectancy theory, adapted from Vroom (1964).

degree and likely be enhanced. If it does not feel fair, then demotivation will be the result.

So, as managers, we can see that the link between effort and performance must be supported with adequate training, instruction, and resources and that the link between performance and rewards and the performance standards applied, must be made clear. It is important in this context to recognise, as set out by Herzberg, that monetary reward is a hygiene factor and that the reward to which expectancy theory refers is the total reward including pay and fringe benefits, as well as the design of jobs and experience of work (recognition, autonomy, work-life balance, personal development), and the organisation culture and physical work environment, etc. In other words, the term reward refers to everything, Herzberg's Hygiene and Motivator factors, which the worker values.

Expectancy Theory, like Herzberg's Two Factor Theory, gives the manager a set of levers they can pull to create and maintain a motivated workforce. It is a practical approach to the problem of individual organisational behaviour. The following section sets out one example of how expectancy theory can be applied in thinking through how to design jobs so that they are as motivating as possible, of course, bearing in mind that this is not sufficient in itself to create motivation as there must also be adequate training, direction, and supply of resources.

THE JOB CHARACTERISTICS MODEL

The job characteristics model developed by Hackman and Oldham[7] is an application of expectancy theory intended to assist the process of job enrichment and thereby to enhance motivation. It is more normally thought of as a tool of HRM rather than managers in general, but its value lies in the way it brings to light the practical things that managers could be doing, themselves, for their people. The model sets out the links between the features of jobs, the individual's experience, and outcomes in terms of motivation. A motivating job leads to high levels of job satisfaction and high levels of job performance. The key factors proposed by the model are listed here:

- *Skill variety*: the extent to which a job makes use of different skills and abilities.
- *Task identity*: the extent to which a job involves a 'whole' and meaningful piece of work.
- *Task significance*: the extent to which a job affects the work of others.

- *Autonomy*: the extent to which a job provides independence and discretion.
- *Feedback*: the extent to which performance information is relayed back to the individual.

Hackman and Oldham propose that improvements in the first three will lead to a perception of the work done as meaningful while improvements in autonomy give the worker a feeling of personal responsibility for outcomes, and improved feedback enables the worker to have a clear knowledge of the outcomes and to be able to measure them for themselves. If we apply expectancy theory to this, we can see that there will be improvements in motivation provided that the rewards are felt to be fair in relation to the effort required. What then are the practical things that the manager can do to help achieve this? Hackman and Oldham suggest, e.g., combining related tasks into a single job rather than excessive differentiation of work. Also, combining workers together into naturally related work units (i.e., into teams, see Chapter 5), providing for mutual support and a share in overall responsibility for outcomes. Of course, all managers should always be seeking to give the fullest and most immediate feedback possible.

REBECCA RAWNSLEY – A MODERN MANAGEMENT CAREER

Q My first question is to know whether you have faced difficulties with motivation? Either the motivation of other people or your own?

So, from personal perspective, yes. My CV tells a story about how my length of time at organisations has sometimes been quite short. Once I feel that I have achieved everything I can, if there is no other activity, nothing more for me to transform, if everything is working perfectly then I personally know that I am done, and it is time move on. There are other times when I start to struggle, start to get demotivated. This is often when there is a lack of senior leadership steer. When it is not clear what we are trying to achieve. Personally, I need to understand, to know clearly what we're trying to do. Also, when there is a lack of leadership it makes my bid management role a lot harder. It becomes tough to get the buy in and commitment needed from everyone involved in bid creation and I must find different workarounds. But I think, as I said, earlier in my career, I just moved at the point where I had excelled because I was not challenged anymore. However, now from a more senior position I can, to some extent, navigate the organisation to adopt different routes and to find new opportunities. So, for me, motivation is about being busy and challenged. Then I am good. From the point of view of my team, I have seen a lot of examples of people feeling undervalued and so being demotivated. Sometimes people view bid management as an admin support activity, low status, therefore. As for individual motivation, for me it is about understanding what each person is after, what is driving them. Money? Status? A change? Progression? Then I can work with them to tailor specific development plans.

Q What do you find the most common source of demotivation?

I should say it is very often people being actively demotivated by the behaviours in an organisation. For example, I think there is often a lot of fatigue over constant change. They have been told they are fantastic then they are moved to some other part of the organisation. They are told this is great new opportunity, you should look to do this and that, but then given no support to develop into their new role. This makes people start to think why am I here? What is this? There's sort of a build-up of negativity over a number of occasions.

Q How do you tackle that sort of situation?

I think my answer to that is related to the fact that I seem always to arrive in new places where there is no properly functioning bid team. So, I have it easier in a way I guess, because I get to come in fresh and set the vision and inspire and try to remotivate those team members that I can. I always accept that some people are at a point where they cannot come back, they are so dissatisfied or feel so undervalued that they can see no future for themselves in the team. But I do think that there are ways to deal with the concerns of most people. You know, whether you give them more empowerment, focus on areas of more interest, remove some of the dull and trivial noise, take the admin away, give them specific individual roles that each finds of interest etc. It is necessary always to be clear and honest and set out realistic expectations. There will always be a need for some frank conversations that unpick previous poor messaging.

Q Let us look at specifics, in your current role or a previous role can you take me through a specific case, maybe an individual who was demonstrating a level of demotivation.

So, at Company F for example. I inherited a team where there were challenges due to having imported the North America proposal management model which meant that it did not provide for the full bid management activity as needed here. Lots of the other parts of the organisation had stepped in to find work arounds and so the role of bid management was vastly diluted. They had been reduced to administering the paperwork. When I arrived, I was able then to spend some time by setting up the appropriate structure to support the work and then I started to offer encouragement to the team members. I had some of those frank conversations about some of their skills gaps, being honest and open about what they needed to do so that they could carry themselves a little differently. So that they could be a little bit surer of themselves, of their role and be more open and engaged and start to build some bonds with the other teams around the organisation.

Q So, this was about intervening at the individual level in the team?

Right, but it was also very important also to be doing stakeholder management, building bridges with wider teams and groups in the organisation to get their buy in and support. But then, at the individual level, bringing my team back from complacency, from boredom. That was a real issue, there were not enough things to do to fill in the day because of the reduced size of the team's role. Of course, recognising that skills weren't necessarily in existence in all team members, rather than just being unused, some people needed upskilling and training to be able to take advantage of this more interesting role.

Q Well, so if I understood correctly in that example, bid management so-called had simply become proposal coordination.

Yes, right. And that meant that the skills have been lost, for example a team member in the Middle East had left because she was offered a job for another company which allowed her to undertake the full range of bid management activities. She had felt undervalued, she felt she had been walked over by Sales, treated as admin. This then meant that the team that was left did not have the appropriate skills. Recruiting to replace this loss of staff brought up the standard of the team a bit and this also helped to bring some validation, some credibility to the team's view of itself. I told them that we all need to lift up to this level and that view gradually became the accepted norm, not just a case of Rebecca saying things.

THE CHAPTER EXAMPLE CASE – MEL

Sarah had selected Adam as one of the change agents to help her ensure that the new strategy was implemented successfully from a quality point of view across the whole firm. Adam was the most junior of the four quality managers at MEL. He had come to MEL only a few years ago to replace one of the original MEL employees when he retired. Previously he had worked for BMW at Works Cowley in Oxford. His background at BMW and its reputation for automotive quality had been a key part of his successful application to join MEL.

This change agent role was a challenge Adam was enjoying but he was aware of a real difficulty among his colleagues in the quality team. Surely there must have been indications that the team could have acted upon at a much earlier point, more forcibly alerting more senior management of the need to take corrective action (he was aware that regular reports were provided but they seemed to have had little impact). Why had the team not asked more questions and sought to press the need for action directly on their Director, Joe Coles? Adam felt that there was a real sense of demotivation, how else was he to explain the fact that the team had allowed quality performance gradually to slip until customers felt they were no longer well served?

Adam felt it essential that this was addressed if the new strategy was to be deployed successfully. He felt that Herzberg's two factor model of motivation might be helpful in thinking through the problem he faced.

Box 4.1 Herzberg

Motivators relate to job content and **hygiene factors** relate to job context.

- **Motivator factors**: aspects of work which lead to high levels of satisfaction and related motivation and performance, including achievement, recognition, responsibility, advancement, growth, and the work itself.
- **Hygiene factors**: aspects of work which remove dissatisfaction, but do not contribute to motivation and performance, including pay, company policy, supervision, status, security, and physical working conditions.

The main point here is to recognise that the opposite of being dissatisfied and hence being demotivated is not to be satisfied and so motivated, but rather to be not dissatisfied and that this does not in itself lead to being motivated.

> Equally being dissatisfied reduces or negates the opportunity to be motivated.
>
> Both hygiene factors and motivation factors are important, together, to the creation of a motivated workforce and thus always need management attention.

Turning first to the hygiene factors, Adam saw that most of them seemed to be strong in MEL, which was widely regarded as a well-run organisation. However, he felt that the quality team was not accorded the status it ought to be in the organisation given the importance its role had in meeting customer needs. Sarah had pointed out to him how important was the ability of MEL to give speedy, on-time, on-specification, and right first-time service to its motorsport customers. MEL's Nuclear Industry and Defence Industry customers certainly felt the same way, although their demands were typically not so urgent. Over time, this lack of perceived status would certainly lead to a team that was increasingly dissatisfied with its lot and hence much less motivated than otherwise might be the case. How might this be addressed?

Reviewing motivation factors, Adam saw the following: -

- Achievement and Recognition – these are related to the status point above; the senior management need explicitly to recognise and praise the important work of the quality team.
- Responsibility – this would seem to be met, the quality team was fully responsible for all aspects of the TQM system as well as the monitoring of the actual quality produced.
- Advancement and Growth – opportunities are, inevitably, limited in a small organisation such as MEL. Reward linked to improvements in quality metrics might provide a temporary way to help here. But this would require expert help from an HR specialist advisor.
- Work itself – while complex and perhaps intrinsically satisfying for those who chose this career path the work tended not to provide task identity, that is involvement in a 'whole' and meaningful piece of work.

Given the importance of quality to customer needs and the strong culture of worker participation at MEL and that all employees are firmly linked into the broader customer network via regular customer feedback briefings there was the opportunity already to enhance the visibility and role of the quality team. This would also provide a significant enhancement of the internal status of the team. These thoughts might need to be enabled or perhaps could best be optimised by some review of the organisational design of MEL (see Chapter 6).

CHAPTER CASE – GARDEN PRODUCTS LIMITED (GPL)

GPL is a business manufacturing wooden garden products such as fencing, planters, simple furniture etc. It is in a commercial wood saw-mill belonging to a large farm in the Kent countryside, GPL is wholly owned by the owners of the farm, Mr, and Mrs Giles. The mill itself was established well over 100 years ago and is housed in one of the farm buildings. Tom Jones is the manager of GPL. There are 20 other GPL employees; two are supervisors and four are general workers. The remaining 14 employees are skilled and semi-skilled machine operators.

GPL has been making a small loss for several years, but this has not previously been a concern in the context of the larger scale operations of the farm, but farm income is now under pressure and GPL must start to pay its way. However, gross margins have been reducing each year, even though wages are low. Also, although the equipment that GPL uses is simple it is old and like the mill building itself the costs of running it are more than would be the case for a modern sawmill of similar capacity. The reduction in overall operating margins is gradually worsening the commercial position of GPL year by year.

There has been little investment at the mill in recent years and productivity has declined. There is an atmosphere of low and worsening staff morale and there has been a growing level of sickness absence. This may have been made worse by the ageing workforce, but Tom felt that this was not the whole story. Although he had been the manager for only 12 months and had been recruited from a modern sawmill most of the staff had worked at the farm, if not actually at the mill, their entire working lives now averaging 35 years. Tom had found it difficult to get new ideas accepted and the thought that GPL must now make a profit seemed to have had little impact on the way that work was done.

The old mill building had been of an excellent design in 1890 and had been well built so that its basic fabric remained sound. However, access was difficult from the main road and the facilities for storage of materials and finished goods were very limited other than in an open yard next to the dairy.

To try to improve productivity and to help bring the mill into profit Tom has invested £500,000 in two state-of-the-art laser guided saws and two computerised turning and finishing machines. The new machinery will be delivered in just a few weeks, and he plans that it will be fully operational within three months. Tom will then be able to update the product range, offering more sophisticated and much higher margin garden and domestic products so as gradually to replace the existing range of rough and relatively unfinished "rustic" products. The new products would include items made from exotic and expensive imported wood largely replacing the use of local materials.

The area around the mill includes many villages where individual very large houses and estates of up-market medium-size houses have been built in recent years. Although the recent economic difficulties have caused new building to slow it is generally anticipated that, within the next 5 years, up to 5,000 new houses will have been built within 20 miles of the farm. Tom believes that the householders will constitute a ready market for his new products, and he plans to provide retail facilities at the mill.

Mr and Mrs Giles have told Tom that they have been happy to make this investment, but they expect to see the business starting to make an operating profit within 12 months. Unfortunately, the Company Cl they have put into the mill recently and the downturn in farm income mean that there is now very little in reserve. They have no further family assets available and there is little cash at the bank.

Source: Authors own practice

CASE DISCUSSION QUESTIONS

Tom has noted in the case that "there is an atmosphere of low and worsening staff morale and there has been a growing level of sickness absence".

1. What would you suggest to Tom as the likely reasons for this?
2. What could you suggest as possible remedies?
3. Comment, in this regard, on Tom's plans for the Mill.

CLASS DISCUSSION QUESTIONS

1. Why is the study of motivation important to successful organisational management?
2. What is the relationship between Maslow's Hierarchy of Needs and Herzberg's two factor theory. Are they interchangeable?
3. What problems can be seen in the equity theory approach to motivation?
4. Explain how the Job Characteristics model is an application of Expectancy Theory

CHAPTER SUMMARY

In this chapter, we have considered how, in an organisational management context, we can develop understanding of how people are likely to behave in different circumstances and to be able to understand when people will work well and work hard, when they will persist, when they will struggle to overcome obstacles and when will people willingly do more than the minimum required by the demands of contract or discipline or social pressure?

The theoretical approaches to this outlined in the chapter were as follows.

- Maslow's theory of human motivation and needs
- Equity theory
- Herzberg's two factor theory of motivation
- Expectancy theory
- The job characteristics model

We concluded that practicing managers, as opposed to theoreticians, would most likely focus on Herzberg's two factor theorem and on expectancy theory because these offer real managerial tools with which to tackle the task of generating, enhancing, and maintaining motivation.

NOTES

1 Maslow, A.H. (1943) A theory of human motivation. *Psychological Review*, 50(4): 370–396.
2 Adams, J.S. (1963) Towards an understanding of inequity. *The Journal of Abnormal and Social Psychology*, 67(5): 422–436.
3 Buchanan, D.A. and Huczynski, A.A. (2019) *Organizational Behaviour* (10th Ed.), Harlow: Pearson.
4 Herzberg, F. (1959) *The Motivation to Work* (2nd Ed.), New York: Wiley.
5 Buchanan, D.A. and Huczynski, A.A. (2019) *Organizational Behaviour* (10th Ed.), Harlow: Pearson.
6 Vroom, V.H. (1964) *Work and Motivation*, New York: John Wiley.
7 Hackman, J.R., Oldham, G., Janson, R. and Purdy, K. (1975) A New Strategy for Job Enrichment. *California Management Review*, 17(4): 57–71.

5 Understanding Group and Team Behaviour

INTRODUCTION

Organisations consist of individuals, but they do not usually work solely as individuals. Every organisation consists of suborganisations usually referred to as groups or teams. These are then assembled into bigger suborganisations with names such as department or division (see Chapter 6). So, what can we expect of the collective behaviour of these groups? How do the motivations of the individual members interact to form the overall behaviour of the group? Are there aspects of group behaviour which arise from the existence of the group rather than solely from its membership? What are the key factors at work here? Understanding all this will enable us to think about how group behaviour can be anticipated and group performance improved.

TYPES OF GROUPS AND FACTORS AFFECTING GROUP PERFORMANCE

One should first notice that there are several different types of groups to be found in the workplace. Some of these are formal in the sense that they have been set up deliberately within the organisational context to carry out specified tasks. Typically, they have terms of reference and a membership which is defined, and a degree of longevity assured by the replacement of members as individuals change. They may meet frequently at regular, rather short intervals such as a project team (such groups are sometimes called Primary Formal Groups) or much less frequently and often be composed of many disparate members such as a large governance committee (sometimes called a Secondary Formal Group).

DOI: 10.4324/9781032686592-5

However, there are very many more, heavily overlapping and interlocking informal groups both primary, such as friends who meet regularly after work or while travelling to work and secondary such as an extensive but rarely or never meeting, network of people with shared interests or similar backgrounds.[1] Formal groups have the power to take decisions and commit resources subject to their terms of reference, but informal groups are very influential behind the scenes potentially determining the attitudes and opinions of individual members even when they are working within the formal groups. The degree to which this is the case will depend on the organisational culture and even the broader context of national culture (see Chapter 6) and other factors such as the age and size and sector of the organisation.

All groups, of whatever type, are influenced in how they behave and perform by some general considerations such as size, task, and composition. Each of these can lead to the development of some general guidance around group formation.

- As a group becomes bigger, it can have within it a broader range of skills and experience but equally the opportunity for individuals to excel is reduced thus reducing individual motivation (see Chapter 4); it is often said that five to six members is ideal, but this depends on how long established is the group and how experienced the members are such that older more experienced groups can be larger as they tend to be self-coordinating and motivating. But larger groups will also include subgroups, friendship groups and groups with shared interests, which will, to some degree, work towards hidden agendas.
- The task itself must be realistically achievable and seen as important however, if it is too easy there will be demotivation. A task which is just sufficiently challenging leads to overall better performance.
- The group must be given access to all the resources it needs and must have the overt support of more senior figures in the organisation. Lack of these is very damaging to morale and effectiveness as is a lack of external peer recognition, acceptance, and approval, whereas, if these exist, this leads to motivation.
- The composition of a group is crucial, between them, members must have all the necessary skills.
- Homogeneous groups in which members share similar values and beliefs produce higher levels of satisfaction and less conflict. But they tend also to be less creative and produce a pressure for conformity. Over time, groups that start out as heterogenous,

unless they are too large, will grow together and become more homogenous. People who work together tend over time to adopt a common unquestioned approach to tasks and to ignore contrary indications; Janis (1972)[2] called this "groupthink", a situation in which cohesive 'in-groups' let the desire for unanimity override sound judgement when generating and evaluating alternative courses of action.

RESPONSES TO GROUPTHINK

Janis identified several observable symptoms of the existence of group-think. As the manager of a group, it would be important to watch for these in the knowledge that it will certainly develop in any group over time. Sometimes, this will happen rather quickly. Symptoms include:

- An exaggerated sense of the importance of the group.
- The group has a sense of invulnerability, tending to take excessive risks based on past success.
- The group appears unanimous in its views as it adopts the views of the most vocal members.
- The group rationalises away decision or interpretation options which fall outside its norms.
- The group asserts that its own position is morally superior and believe that they, as moral individuals, are unlikely to make bad decisions.
- The group negatively stereotypes its competitors as wrong, weak, or evil.
- The group pressures its members to conform, imposing sanctions on those who express doubts or question the validity of group beliefs.
- Members of the group censor and try to minimise their own doubts rather than express a non-conforming opinion.

What then should a manager do when groupthink presents itself? Two approaches exist, firstly to disrupt the homogeneity of the group and secondly, to improve the group's decision-making techniques to provide some checks and balances to the tendency to make only conforming decisions. Disrupting the homogeneity of the group might be done by adding members or changing the existing membership, perhaps on a regular basis if the group is intended to be long lived. But either of these might be difficult to achieve in the light of costs involved, loss of expertise, limited access to appropriate skills or the risks of making the group overlarge and reducing group performance. However, group decision making might also be improved by the introduction of formal decision-making techniques such as these:

- Brainstorming – members offer as many ideas as they can think of before any discussion or evaluation takes place.
- Nominal group technique – as above but final choice is made by secret independent vote or ranking.
- Dialectical inquiry – two subgroups develop different positions and then debate to find an agreed position.
- Devil's advocacy – a group member is nominated to critique the group position by a process of advocating an opposing view, testing, and enhancing the eventual decision.
- Red/Blue team review – an outside group (red) is set up to critique and test the group's (blue) draft position and the final decision is based on the outcome.

GROUP STRUCTURAL DEVELOPMENT AND TEAMS

All groups of people have an internal structure. This is both a function of and interacts with, the power and cultural patterns of the organisation within which they exist (see Chapter 7). The structure created results in differences between the people in the group across several fronts such as status, power, and role and everyone will develop a known position in the group structure. A further complication is that the structure of the group will depend also on the processes occurring within the group such as how decisions are made and how problems are tackled. Equally, the reality of the internal processes will depend on the structure, for example, the methods adopted by a leader and the leader's ideas will come to dominate. This topic area will be considered in more depth in the light of the ideas on emergent organisational properties covered in Chapter 7.

Groups start out as just a collection of people who do not know each other and may know little or nothing about the task at hand. There is then a natural process of development during which the structure discussed above emerges. A model of how this development happens was set out by Tuckman and Jensen in 1977.[3] They talk of four stages in development, Forming, Storming, Norming, and Performing. The first three of these are to do with the creation of an effective group structure capable of undertaking the task:

- In the *forming* stage group members become familiar with each other, starting out in a state of confusion and uncertainty. Individuals are assessing the situation and each other.
- In the *storming* stage there is disagreement and tension amongst group members, cliques form, there is disagreement over priorities and a struggle for leadership roles.
- In the *norming* stage the group becomes coherent as consensus is achieved, standards are agreed, trust emerges, and leadership is accepted.

The fourth, performing, stage is that in which the group becomes a team:

- In the *performing* stage the group becomes wholly focused on the tasks in hand and exhibits a very high level of goal orientation.

TEAMS AND TEAM MANAGEMENT

Teams are special groups in which members have regular contact, coordinated activities, approach their objective jointly, share responsibility, and support each other. A useful definition of the term is that a team is a small number of people with complementary skills who are committed to a common goal and approach for which they hold themselves mutually accountable.[4] Teams may be found anywhere in an organisation with very many different roles and goals but commonly occurring types are those which are focused within one functional activity (e.g. business to business marketing), those which cut across functions to provide organisational benefit (e.g. a product development team), those set up to solve a particular problem (a project team) and virtual teams, which may be any of the above types, dealt with at more length below.

The key point to be observed from Tuckman and Jensen's model is that groups must pass through these stages to become teams and it is for the manager to ensure that this happens successfully, facilitating each step. Equally, if something happens to disrupt the team, such as the loss of a member or a requirement to make a radical change of direction then it will be necessary for the group to work through some or all the stages again.

We can perhaps all imagine the concerns and difficulties we are likely to face in managing teams in our workplace, but it is useful to have a list so that we can get ahead and be sure we are aware of these issues and perhaps can deal with them before problems arise. The following list has been developed by Schneider and Barsoux (2003),[5] and it is recommended that managers of teams review this material as a process of audit of their management practice.

Creating a sense of purpose, what is the team mission? Have clear goals and objectives been set? Are any objectives that have been set SMART,[6] i.e. specific, measurable, achievable, realistic, and time-bound:

- Specific – there is a clear statement of what is required.
- Measurable – so that progress can be monitored and to know when the objective has been achieved.
- Achievable – challenging but ensuring that failure is not built in. Objectives should be agreed explicitly between managers and teams to ensure commitment.
- Relevant – focused on outcomes that are clearly relevant to achieving the overall mission.
- Time-bound – include an explicitly agreed date by which the outcome must be achieved.

Structuring the task, what tasks are to be accomplished, who will do them, and by when? What priorities can be set between the various tasks? How will the work be divided up, what will be the roles and responsibilities of the different team members? Who will be the team leader (see also Chapter 8)?

Building the team, is there trust and mutual understanding between the team members? If the team is international or multicultural, what shall be the working language? How can we ensure the participation of all members? How is conflict managed? The answers to these questions and others must emerge as the team passes through the four Tuckman and Jensen stages of group development.

Success in building an effective team will mean that everyone on the team feels able to have a voice in the work of the team and how it is performed. They feel able to ask for help and to admit to any mistakes just as much as they feel able to suggest ideas and to point out difficulties. This sense of comfort, inclusion, and trust is often termed psychological safety.[7]

VIRTUAL TEAM WORKING

If, as increasingly is the case, the team operates virtually or in a hybrid format then special attention must be given to questions around the feasibility of at least some face-to-face meetings and to the building of trust and interdependence despite the limited interpersonal contacts.

From our understanding of individual motivation, it appears likely also that the differences between real, hybrid, and virtual working environments will impact both hygiene and motivation factors. It seems likely that it will help maintain motivation, to the benefit of the organisation, through team-based work, socialisation, and collaboration if as many meetings as possible are held in person. Equally, it is clear that the modern workplace has changed since the pandemic of 2020/2021 and is unlikely to return to its former style. Managers ought therefore to embrace the benefits associated with hybrid working through open communication and personal connection with employees, to ensure that hybrid working becomes embedded successfully in organisational culture and aligns with the organisation's goals.

DIVERSITY AND INCLUSION

As we have seen above, the makeup of groups is very important to their operation. Clearly, one aspect of this is the individual make-up of the organisation as a whole, i.e., its diversity. This term refers to the mixture of attributes within a workforce that in significant ways affect how people think, feel, and behave at work, and their acceptance, work performance, satisfaction, or progress in the organisation.[8] Or more simply, diversity has also been described as the varied perspectives and approaches to work that members of different identity groups bring.[9]

Thinking about the impact of diversity in an organisation we might conclude that there are likely to be problems to be faced around a discrimination and fairness perspective calling for a focus on justice and the fair treatment of all members of the organisation, as a moral imperative. Equally, we might expect some benefits such as where differences are thought to create opportunities such as access to new markets or consumers recognising that markets are of course, culturally diverse so that matching this in our own workforce would seem a good way of gaining access and legitimacy to those markets. Also, the skills, experiences, and insights of diverse employees offer a valuable, wider, resource for organisational learning, innovation, and change.

However, such benefits will not accrue, and neither can the moral imperative be met unless the diverse workforce is fully involved across all aspects of the work of the organisation. This is the challenge of inclusion that is, encouraging participation and moving beyond merely appreciating diversity, towards leveraging, and integrating diversity into everyday work life. Several aspects of human behaviour will operate to make this difficult and these aspects are likely to be enhanced in groups of people who tend to groupthink. These include the following all of which must expressly be guarded against:

- Stereotyping – over-generalising about a particular group or category of people
- Unconscious bias – the potential for prejudice is hard-wired into human cognition
- Ignorance
- Lack of empathy
- Political correctness

By employing people who reflect their substantive customer base, that is their largest market, and who also reflect the make-up of their key supplier firms, it is likely that the organisation will benefit operationally. By doing this it will have enhanced the degree to which it has the right resources and capabilities. An important impact will also be to foster innovation through diversity of thought process. It has been observed over many years (see Adler[10]) that the potential for superior performance of culturally diverse groups is high because of their breadth of resources, insights, perspectives, and experiences that better enable creativity and innovation.

THE IMPACT OF DIVERSITY ON TEAMWORK

Diverse teams should therefore have great impact for better performance but managing such teams is difficult. Mistrust, misunderstanding, miscommunication, stress, and a lack of cohesion can often negate the potential benefits of diversity to the team. When functioning effectively, multicultural teams use their diversity to generate multiple perspectives, problem definitions, ideas, action alternatives, and solutions. They will have learnt to achieve consensus despite diversity; and to balance the need for creativity and cohesion on an ultimate solution.

Adler gives lists of the advantages and disadvantages of working with multicultural teams.

Advantages

- Diversity permits increased creativity through having a wide range of perspectives leading to more and better ideas. A particular advantage of diversity is that groupthink is less likely to occur.
- Enhanced concentration is required to understand others in the team, leading to an improved level of discussion and

idea generation as meanings are clarified across the cultural differences. Combined with increased creativity, this will result in better problem definition, more alternative solutions, and better decisions.

- Multicultural teams can therefore be more productive and more effective.

Disadvantages

- Diversity causes a lack of cohesion around mistrust and miscommunication. This creates stress in the team members, producing tension and an inability constructively to discuss situations, ideas, and solutions.
- It becomes difficult to agree when agreement is needed and difficult to gain consensus on decisions.
- As a result, multicultural teams can become less efficient, effective, and productive.

Managers of such teams should seek to press the advantages and avoid the disadvantages – but how? Adler concludes that multicultural teams perform better than monocultural ones in identifying problems and generating alternatives, but this depends crucially on the team leadership and on its attitudes to diversity and differences of opinion. A leader who ignores or seeks to suppress cultural differences becomes an obstacle to team performance whereas a leader who acknowledges and embraces the cultural differences turns these differences into an asset. The former leader will depress team performance below average whereas the latter will elevate team performance above average.

REBECCA RAWNSLEY – A MODERN MANAGEMENT CAREER

Q how important is the management of teams in your bid management role?

There are two aspects to this, my bid management team and the broader groups involved in the overall process. Firstly, the bid team, management of this is obviously very important. We must provide a standard of services that are not individually dependent. So, it is important to make sure that everyone in the team is aligned and happy and not sending out an unhappy message of frustration. I must ensure that there is consistency and that then helps to manage future bids because we will have set the standard expectation. At the level of the other groups involved around the organisation, these are our internal customers, there is only so much that I can do but it is around the stakeholder, the messaging, the internal communications, and that is where I need the team to back each other up to start to represent the bid team as a unified whole.

Q So if you had a team that was not working in this way how would you set about rebuilding such a team that was failing.

So, first, after my years in the role I know that there are common pitfalls and challenges. It does not take too long to identify these pitfalls, but I always start with observation. I want to see as many bids in action as possible across as many different sectors, sales team, product teams, solution teams etc. I am looking to see how people interact, to see what is expected of each other and how the team are engaged. So, monitor and observe, through sitting quietly, even that if that means watching a bid fail just so that I can diagnose the situation. Of course, this can create a lot of upset. Questions are asked, what is she looking for, what is going on? Often there is a perception that roles are being reduced in other areas by a bid management team coming in. So, I almost need to let people prove my point. So first, I observe I watch, I take copious notes. I then map what I see against the bid management lifecycle built from the customer procurement life cycle. This is to prove that it is not just me being awkward. And then I start to pick out key characters from the team that are potential influencers, the loud voices, the ones to whom people listen. So, that is picking those that are the actual decision makers, even if that is not in their formal not job role.

Q So, you are rebuilding the team by observing what everybody can and does do, and then picking the ones that have the required capabilities and skills.

Yeah, from within the team, that is right, but also on a wider basis as well, the rest of the group. People are usually quite open to being involved and to discuss all this because usually, by bringing in a proper bid management process, they can solve a lot of their constant challenges. It doesn't take too much of a chat to say, you know, I've been involved in this at other organisations, and this is what I have seen elsewhere and now I've just been watching to see how it goes here. The idea is to share with them a couple of key thoughts and get their views on this and be seen to be treating the views of everyone seriously. Then I run pilots and to validate the pilot with everyone I get senior stakeholder support. I do not impose things in a peremptory fashion. I always work from the bottom up. But then I am also targeting the top to get buy in from the leadership. Whichever leaders are the ones that count in the organisation they need to be seen to be backing the project and setting the tone around the importance of what is being done.

Q OK. So how long does this take?

I would say you can see two people timelines. Longer term, but within a year, you can see significant change and really overhaul the process. Within three months, you should start to see the quick wins, you can start to see some real changes and that's then freeing people up outside the bid team to focus on their own areas, their real work. There will be evidence, which I make a point of capturing, which will show, within three months, a picture starting to improve. A build-up of enthusiasm for the new bid management team will begin to emerge.

Q Suppose we were talking about the marketing team or a product development team or even an operational team in the field would some of those same approaches work?

Yes, I think so. You must observe because you don't want to be making rash assumptions. That would be arrogant and obnoxious, leading to real problems. It would be a situation in which things were done without any context, background or understanding. I have had change done to me in that way. It does not matter the extent to which there are briefing sessions, staff communications updates, bombardment with emails if there is no real engagement with the people affected. Yeah. You should observe and then validate by talking it through with those involved. Do this straight away. Do not leave it for months, talk it through and ask questions. This will generate interest in what you are doing and what you are changing and then more people will want to be involved. In general, there is no need to rush. We need to go slow and steady. To convince people and get them to come in to help you; instead of fighting uphill.

Q Now, does that same way of thinking also apply not so much to your own team but also to your stakeholders' groupings? I know you would hope to have the support of top management to improve the bid management function in the way you're describing this, but is that normally the case? Do top management understand the importance of bid management?

> I think typically not. No. They think the sales team are the key and bid management is often the overlooked part of any win. But I've always managed to get it to that point. I always ask where we can elevate our position, where we can raise our profile. I think that's important and then you can make some serious headway.

Q Do you think there should be a director of bidding? That it should be part of the most senior level of executive management?

> At board level, I would argue yes. I wonder if we'll ever see it. For now, I think a good step would be to merge a little bit more with strategy. Or perhaps to be recognised as a key top-level department of the Directorate of Sales. It is the case that a lot of organisations are realising the value of the data and the metrics and the insights that a bid function can bring. It is perhaps a matter of professionalising the function.

Q That is interesting and it seems to me that you could make the case that as the bid manager, you have probably got knowledge of and access to a more complete view of the whole firm than almost anybody else apart from the chief executive?

> I would say that was the case in smaller organisations, but I think as you get into bigger organisations perhaps not. There are lots of layers and lots of people and lots to know.

Q To what extent does the bid team need to include people who are knowledgeable about the specific product that is to be sold?

> Every time. Every time. If you are bidding, you need to have the solution built by the experts from the different parts of the organisation. You need a representative of each subject matter expertise area. Whereas, our expertise is the procurement process compliance, how to leverage the organisational capabilities to fit with the customer needs, accessing and bringing together that broader team, and keeping them on track.

THE CHAPTER EXAMPLE CASE – MEL

While analysing the situation at MEL Sarah had formed the view that there was a problem around a lack of new blood and a lack of sources of new ideas in MEL. This, she thought, was especially the case in Production and perhaps, she thought privately, in the management team too. Reflecting upon this she realised that the fundamental issue to address was the management team, including as it did the Director of Production. It was clear to her that the management team had displayed symptoms of Groupthink. She had seen.

- They had a sense of invulnerability, tending to take excessive risks based on past success.
- They appeared unanimous in their views adopting the views of the most vocal members.
- They rationalised away decision or interpretation options which were outside the norm.

However, this problem would not be an easy matter to deal with; internal stresses would arise. These would be likely to result in overt and potentially damaging political behaviour (see Chapter 8). Also, she knew that none of the current team had any personal interest in selling their share of the firm or retiring. Nevertheless, a way had to be found to bring fresh ideas to the decision makers at MEL. Perhaps a reorganisation could set up a situation in which new people would naturally become involved? Or perhaps a reorganisation that opened a new role which could be filled by external recruitment might be considered (see Chapter 6), perhaps a Quality Services Director?

But even if such changes could be achieved would these be sufficient in themselves to address the lack of new thinking in the Production area of MEL? Perhaps not and the age structure of the area combined with the immediacy of the problems emerging around quality and customer satisfaction called for an urgent response. The thought that occurred to Sarah was of some sort of programme of remedial recruitment. This could be designed to lower the average age, but it could also maintain the depth of knowledge and experience inherent in each team by allowing the opportunity for it to be passed on before the older members of staff suddenly retired. Of course, all of this would require significant investment. Perhaps the first element of this investment would be for Sarah to seek input on this from an HR specialist to act as a consultant to her change project.

Sarah realised that significant organisational change and the bringing in of new people, at whatever level, would disrupt the existing teams. This would have benefits in relation to stemming the growth of groupthink, but it would certainly require a definite effort around team building.

CHAPTER CASE – GROUPTHINK EMERGES IN A US ELEMENTARY SCHOOL

Efforts were being made by staff in a US elementary school to improve standards of literacy by trialling new approaches and lesson types. The group were giving up their own time to contribute to an effort which they felt important. Initially, these trials had the support of the school principal but then, part way through the school year, the principal changed his policy, insisting on teaching returning to previous standards of detailed lesson planning and the previously used weekly testing regime. No reason for this was offered. The staff team complained but acquiesced in the abandonment of their short-term plans. In their ongoing discussion, however, they appeared overwhelmed and incapable of responding appropriately and adequately to the difficulties they now faced in pursuing their goals. During group discussion, they regularly talked over each other, they strayed from whatever topic happened to be on the table at a given time; and their talk rarely led to any purposeful planning. When the group did form plans, follow-through became an issue. Members seemed to look to each other for moral support via expressions of sympathy. The staff repeatedly expressed the problems they saw with the tests and related instruction, but no clear goals emerged from their discussion. Those who suggested some form of "rebellion" against the principal's decision failed to follow this up in a form of self-censorship. In the end, the teachers simply accepted the reversion in policy, rationalising that the focus on testing was probably good for their students. An observer studying the work of the group of staff felt that the members were demonstrating symptoms of psychological stress which had undermined the teachers' ability to manage the situation effectively.

Adapted from: Not the Desired Outcome: Groupthink Undermines the Work of a Literacy Council. *Small Group Research* 2020, 51(4): 517–541.

CASE DISCUSSION QUESTIONS

1. What is the cause of the group's inability to move forward or to support their beliefs against opposition?
2. Is this a case of groupthink? Which of Janis' symptoms can be seen in the case?

CLASS DISCUSSION QUESTIONS

1. What do you understand about the term "Groupthink". Does this concept have any importance for our understanding of Teams?
2. Tuckman and Jensen describe a model of team formation. What are the main elements of the model? Apply the model to a work or other team environment with which you are familiar.
3. Explain why it is that multicultural teams are thought likely to be better performing or worse performing than average.
4. How might you set about ensuring that a new virtual team would be likely to be effective?

CHAPTER SUMMARY

- The fundamental part of an organisation is people working in groups, from pairs through to the whole organisation.
- Groups are both formal, set up by the organisation, and informal naturally occurring social groups.
- The performance of a group is impacted by size, task, resources, and composition.
- A homogeneous composition can lead to group failure through Groupthink.
- Groupthink may be addressed by disrupting the homogeneity of a group and by introducing formal decision-making processes to deflect the negative aspects of Groupthink.
- Teams are special groups in which members have regular contact, coordinated activities, approach their objective jointly, share responsibility, and support each other.
- Teams that are diverse in their membership have the capacity to be higher performing than average subject to that diversity being embraced by the team and especially by the team leader.

NOTES

1 Kakabadse, A., Ludlow, R. and Vinnicombe, S. (1988) *Working in Organizations*, Harmondsworth: Penguin.
2 Janis, I.L. *(1972) Victims of Groupthink: A Psychological Study of Foreign-Policy Decisions and Fiascos*, Boston, MA: Houghton Mifflin.

3 Tuckman, B.W. and Jensen, M.A.C. (1977) Stages of small group development revisited. *Group and Organizational Studies*, 2(4): 419–427.
4 Francesco, A.M. and Gold, B.A. (2005) *International Organisational Behaviour*, Upper Saddle River, NJ: Pearson/Prentice Hall.
5 Schneider, S.C. and Barsoux, J.-L. (2003) *Managing across Cultures*, Harlow: Pearson Education.
6 Doran, G.T. (1981) There's a S.M.A.R.T. way to write management's goals and objectives. *Management Review*, 70(11): 35–36.
7 Edmondson, A. (1999) Psychological safety and learning behaviour in work teams. *Administrative Science Quarterly*, 44(2): 350–383.
8 Nishii, L.H. (2013) The benefits of climate for inclusion for gender-diverse groups. *Academy of Management Journal*, 56(6): 1754–1774.
9 Ely. (1996) Making differences matter: A new paradigm for managing diversity. *Harvard Business Review*, September–October: 79–90.
10 Adler, N.J. (2008) *International Dimensions of Organisational Behaviour*, Mason, OH: Thomson South-Western.

6 Organisational Design

THE STRATEGIC CONTEXT

A recurring theme in organisation design is the question of the alignment or "fit" of the organisation, i.e. its coherence with both the external environment and the organisational goals. The organisation will have, at any given time:

- A specific structure,
- Certain systems of control,
- A set of values and an organisational culture,
- Internal power structures and the political action required to acquire and deploy power,
- Numerous stakeholders of varying power and interest,
- A transformation process which turns inputs into outputs including goods, services, reputation, and waste.
- Resources used in the transformation process which include:
  - A range or physical, financial and intellectual resources and
  - Most crucially, people working within the organisation with certain skills and capabilities and, hopefully, a high level of motivation towards the success of the organisation.

All of this must fit with the organisation's goals and accommodate to a rapidly changing external environment. It may be helpful to diagram the environments as in Figure 6.1.

There is a pressure to organise for efficiency and effectiveness, outlined at the start of Chapter 3, but this must be done in a way which also enables a flexible response to the changing environments, enabling organisational growth and innovation. In the modern economy, there is a high level of competitive pressure along both of these axes.

DOI: 10.4324/9781032686592-6

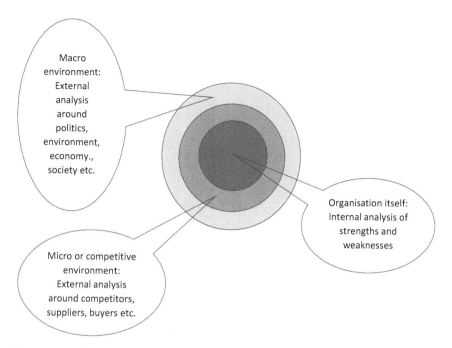

Figure 6.1 The internal, competitive, and macro environments of the organisation.

This leads us to the view that an organisation cannot be in the form of a machine, "Mechanistic" nor cannot it afford to be inefficient by being wholly "Organic" (able to learn and evolve).[1] Rather it has to be both of these things at once, we have termed this "Adaptive" (Figure 6.2).

UNDERSTANDING ORGANISATIONAL DESIGN

The question of organisational design deals with how the building blocks of the organisation, the individuals, groups, and teams discussed in previous chapters, are brought together in a series of complex relationships designed to enable delivery of the organisational objectives. Here one should note that there is a strong link between this topic and organisational strategic decision making. When considering organisational design alongside strategy, one must ask a number of important questions that impact on the organisational thinking covered in this chapter:

- Is the current structure the most appropriate means of organising to meet goals?
- If not, then what organisational changes are required?
- How feasible or workable are these structural alternatives?
- What are the advantages and disadvantages of each alternative?

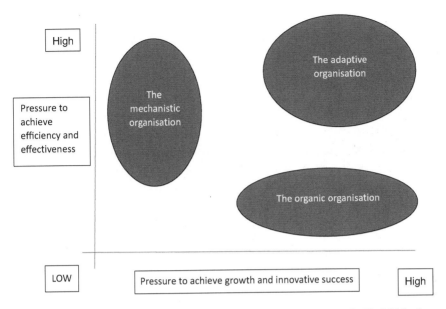

Figure 6.2 The Adaptive Organisation, Cassells, E. and Elsworth, T., 2009 after Roberts, J. *The Modern Firm*, OUP, 2007.

Organisational design thus deals with the actual overall shape of the organisation and is often to be found published in the form of organisation charts including the names and titles of people and groups as well as contact information.

There is no best way to design an organisation. As will be seen below everything depends on the context, on the environment, on the market, on the technology and of course, on the history of the organisation and previous decisions; managers cannot start from anywhere apart from where they are. In other words, everything is situationally contingent. An important contingency that may apply in some limited but high profile cases is the impact of governmental regulation. It is a factor that may have considerable influence over organisation design and structure, e.g., regulations in the UK force banks to ensure clear separation between investment banking and consumer banking thus forcing banks to have an overall structure and design different from what one might otherwise expect.

STRUCTURING THE ORGANISATION

Structuring an organisation is around questions of coordination and control. Deciding on a structure for the organisation requires the making of decisions about the coordination and control of the various subactivities undertaken as part of delivering the overall mission. We will ask whether these subactivities should be based around special expertise and skills or some other factors such as physical location or customer relationships perhaps.

- **Coordination** involves the creation and management of internal information flows to enable effective decision making.
- **Control** involves the appropriate distribution of decision-making rights and authority (i.e., delegation of these from the apex of the organisation to the appropriate location in the organisation).

The purpose here is to ensure that decisions are taken where and by whom they are intended to be; considering the size and importance of the commitment thereby imposed on the organisation and the complexity and dynamism of the context. The larger the size and importance should indicate less delegation and the larger the complexity and dynamism should indicate more delegation.

This location of authority in the organisation may be centralised or decentralised in its nature. Or more likely in a large organisation it will be some unique mixture of the two varying across different parts of the organisation. It is perfectly feasible for authority to be decentralised in some parts of an organisation and highly centralised in others, e.g. a typical university has a highly centralised administrative function but a highly decentralised teaching and research function.

What are the advantages of centralisation or decentralisation as this is a choice the manager will always have to make?

- **Advantages of choosing a centralised structure** include improved uniformity in decisions across the organisation, decisions made at senior level are more likely to be made in awareness of future planning, fewer managers are needed, and simpler planning and reporting procedures needed.
- **Advantages of decentralisation** include faster decision making, decision making that is more accurate in tackling local needs, and it means minor problems can be dealt with locally reducing wasted and often inaccurate internal communication, more junior managers have the chance to develop their decision-making skills and there will be increased creativity, innovation and flexibility.

Turning to the practical details to be considered by the manager when structuring an organisation, five key questions must be addressed.

- **Specialisation** – Should there be high specialisation, or should workers do a wider range of different tasks? Among a range of other factors this will have important impacts on employee motivation.

- **Layers of management** – Should there be many layers in a tall hierarchy or few in a flat hierarchy? Again, this will impact motivation substantially, but also internal communication and consideration must be given to the financial impact of the costs of the relatively higher paid staff involved in a tall hierarchy.
- **Span of control** – How many subordinates should a manager be responsible for; impacting internal communications, decision making speed and motivation.
- **Chain of command and departmentalisation** – should an individual or group report to a manager with comparable specialist knowledge or to a manager with a more holistic view of the organisation and its mission? The former is discussed further below under the heading Functional Structures and the latter under the heading divisional structures. A combination of the two is discussed below under the heading Matrix Structures.
- **Formal systems and operating procedures** – should written rules, records and procedures be used to coordinate and control the activities of different individuals or should this process be left to communications and relationships between people?

It is important for managers to have tools which help think about how best to put an organisation together as well as to review an existing organisation to see if it remains valid in whatever new circumstances are arising. Henry Mintzberg (1979) wrote extensively on this subject and offers the following useful approach.[2]

He proposes that all organisations have the following five basic elements:

- **The strategic apex** – the most senior managers of the organisation, perhaps also the owners in the case of a small organisation.
- **The middle line** – those managers who stand in a direct line management relationship between the strategic apex and the operating core. In a small organisation this element may not be very distinct, if at all, from the strategic apex.
- **The operating core** – produces and delivers the products or services.
- **The technostructure** – experts who design and operate systems to standardise and control workflow and outputs. Again, in a small organisation this may be hard to distinguish from the strategic apex. Also, in any size of organisation, it may be a function largely or completely undertaken by contractors.

- **The support** – those specialists who provide support to the other elements but are not a fundamental part of the workflow such as a human resources team, a marketing team or a Finance and Accounts team. As above this may rather disappear in a small organisation or be a role fulfilled by contractors.

In creating a new organisation or in considering how to reconstruct the organisation as it grows or as circumstances change, we should look to think clearly about how the roles of these five elements will be delivered.

In an existing organisation, if any of these elements appear to be missing or to be too large or too small or to appear to stand in a different relationship than expected to the other elements then there may, perhaps, be flaws in the structural design of the organisation.

In either case typical contingent factors that will need to be considered include as below:

- **The environment** – is it static or dynamic, is it hostile or friendly, is it simple or complex?
- **The age of the organisation** – is it just founded, growing into its product/market, mature have reached a steady relationship with its product/market or old, perhaps declining?
- **The size of the organisation** – is it a few individuals who all know each other well or consisting of a small number of specialised subgroups the leaders of which are directly supervised by the founder or consisting of a large number of subgroups perhaps separated in space as well as specialism, or is it a very large organisation with multiple products in multiple locations?
- **The style or configuration of the organisation** – is it a simple centralised organisation, a bureaucratic formalised organisation, a professional organisation dependant on individual professional judgements, a divisional organisation with each division focused on a product, a market or an operating location, or an ad hoc organisation in which everything changes according to the demands of each project?
- **The key processes required by the product/market** – is it required that the products or services are highly standardised, or do they vary very widely, is it required that the working processes are highly standardised, or do they vary very widely, or is standardisation instead around norms, values, and professional decision making and self-control?

We might also ask whether there are any broad general rules for what makes a good or bad organisational structure and how we might recognise this in our organisation? Work done by Daft[3] (2008) has addressed this by identifying key measures of good organisational performance:

- Organisations are intended to deliver some goal or goals; they have a mission, and this is why they were set up. The strategy of the organisation is the plan or process by which the organisation will deliver those goals. Accordingly, in a good organisation the structure must help in delivering the strategy.
- Organisations are intended to make it easier to deliver the mission than if it was pursued by individuals or disconnected groups. One measure of this is the degree to which the costs of the operation are less for the organisation than they would be without the organisation – the so called "transaction costs". Transaction costs are the total costs of making a transaction, including the cost of planning, deciding, changing plans, resolving disputes, and after-sales. Therefore, the transaction cost is one of the most significant factors in business operation and management[4] and they will be minimised by a good organisational structure.
- Organisations face an external environment that changes continuously and sometimes, very quickly. It is essential that organisations respond well to the demands this makes to survive. A good organisational structure facilitates this.

Daft also identified some observable symptoms of bad organisational structures:

- Bad organisations often display slow decision making or poor-quality decision making and often both. Frequently this is found to originate in poor internal communication systems and a lack of appropriate delegation.
- Bad organisations often fail to respond innovatively to changes in their environment; often due to poor internal coordination and risk aversion being built into the organisational culture.
- Bad organisations often display too much internal conflict as suborganisations and individuals jockey for power and influence at the expense of attending to the organisational mission.

ORGANISATIONAL TYPES

There are many very complex organisation structures in use by organisations large and small. However, they can be categorised into three main types: the unitary or functional structure, the divisional structure, and the matrix structure.

Functional Structure

The functional structure collects all the people working in each type of activity or function, into a specialist suborganisation under the leadership of a senior practitioner of that function. It is particularly suitable for when there are stable conditions in the market and in the broader environment. It is also suitable for a smaller organisation and, typically, at some level of subdivision, even the largest organisations tend towards the functional organisation. The difficulty with the functional structure is that communication tends to occur vertically rather than laterally making for slow information flows across the functions, subject to loss of meaning through multiple levels of transmission. Further the communication that does occur effectively tends to be within specialist silos and so lacking in breadth and recognition of concerns and opportunities elsewhere in the organisation. This imposes a very heavy coordinating load on the strategic apex, especially in times of great environmental dynamism (Figure 6.3).

Divisional Structure

The divisional structure collects all the people working on a particular project or product or service or in a particular location or for a particular customer type into a suborganisation headed by a senior practitioner from that aspect of the organisation. Each division operates in effect, as a stand-alone company doing its own research, production, marketing, etc. Divisional managers are responsible for all operating

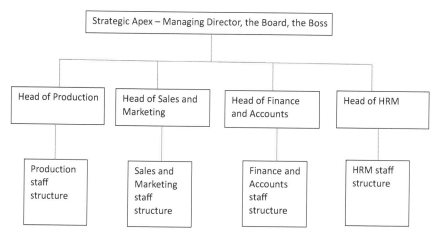

Figure 6.3 A typical functional structure.

decisions while the strategic apex is free to concentrate on broad strategic decisions. Divisional managers compete for funds in a competitive internal Company market based on their operating performance in the past and the future projects they propose. Typically, each division is organised functionally but the focus of the knowledge and experience of the divisional management team on the operational needs of their division combined with the fact that the division is not a functional organisation which has become too large tends to optimise operational decisions. This is, of course, an excellent basis for successful delivery of a good corporate strategy. Thus, the advantage of the divisional structure is that it enables an organisation to grow beyond the size at which the functional organisation would be effective, thus acquiring economies of scale. Having said that, the nature of the division is that it could, in principle, be a separate business and it will compete strongly with the other divisions in the corporation, at best for funds and other resources and at worst in the marketplace. A process of Balkanisation (the fragmentation of an area, country, or region into multiple smaller and hostile units) therefore tends to take place (Figure 6.4).

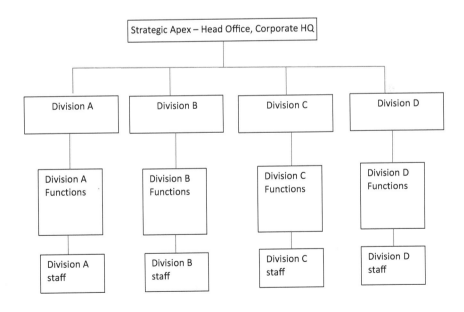

The divisions might focus on a particular project or product or service or on a particular location or customer type or in some complex cases there might be examples of each of these within one

Figure 6.4 A multi divisional structure.

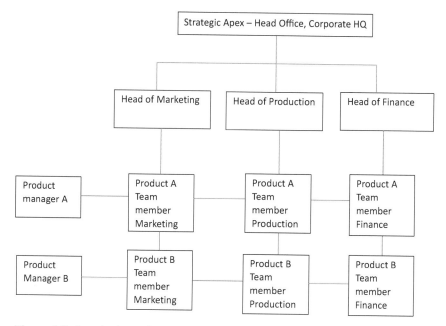

Figure 6.5 A typical matrix structure.

Matrix Structure

The matrix structure is a complex mixture of the two previous structures in which people report both to a senior functional leader and a senior project, product, service, or location leader. Many major organisations adopt a matrix structure so as to provide control over the functional departments, and to allow inter-departmental coordination. The matrix structure comprises employees working in teams composed of employees from different functions units (e.g. marketing, human resources, and production) each contributing to specific projects. Each team member reports therefore to two bosses – their project team manager and their functional manager. This type of organisation is complicated, and it creates a high management overhead and places individual employees in the often difficult position of standing between two bosses with competing priorities. On the other hand, in principle, it overcomes many of the difficulties described above around functional and divisional structures (Figure 6.5).

THE INFORMAL ORGANISATION

It is important to note also that every organisation consists not only of the formal organisation considering all the factors discussed above but also an **informal organisation** made up of the relationships that arise spontaneously between individuals in the workplace as they meet, work together, socialise and form friendships. Employees might well also have outside of work relationships with other people in the organisation and these, of course, form part of the informal organisation.

These relationships between individual employees lead to the development of informal groups each with its own values and norms of behaviour which operate in the same way as the ordinary work groups discussed in previous chapters. The informal organisation is looser and more flexible and more spontaneous but nonetheless very powerful and necessarily heavily relied upon because it meets the personal needs of people.

Successful managers will be fully aware of the informal organisation around their employees and will be fully part of their own informal groups and relationships, often extending outside the organisation. Effective use of the informal organisation in support of the formal one is a sign of management excellence.

DESIGNING THE ORGANISATION

The task of designing an organisation, whether from scratch or to re-develop it, is very complex with many decisions to be made. It is helpful to have a model illustrating the key elements to be considered. One such is the Star model developed by Jay Galbraith.[5] The starting point is the strategy adopted by the organisation which, if it is to be achieved successfully, will require the organisation to have certain capabilities. The creation of these capabilities in the organisation will then depend on four interlocking sets of factors (see Figure 6.6) each of which impacts each of the others to create a complex and delicate organisational balance:

- The structure – determining the location of formal power and authority.
- The processes – the connected activities which move information around in the organisation, the work and management processes which monitor, coordinate and control activities.
- The people practices – the human resources practices for selection, training and development aimed at ensuring the availability of the necessary competences at all levels of the organisation.
- The rewards system – aligning individual and group behaviour and performance with the overall needs of the organisation rather than the narrow desires of the individual or group.

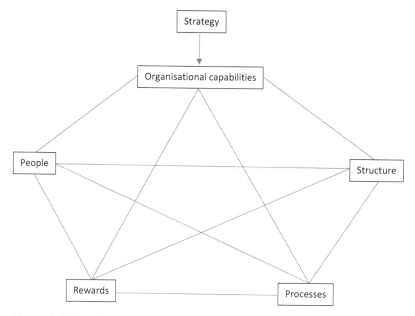

Figure 6.6 The Star model adapted from Galbraith and Kates (2007).

It is worth noting also that strategy will change as the external environment of the organisation develops requiring therefore different capabilities. Thus, an organisation which has the potential to be successful in the long run is one which has additional dynamic capabilities enabling internal change. These are general management capabilities. The following is adapted from Teece's[6] work on this subject:

- **Sensing** – the ability to sense the need for change.
- **Seizing** – the ability to seize, or accept, the need for change.
- **Reconfiguring** – the ability to reconfigure the organisation as necessary, requiring flexibility, creativity, and an innovative ability.

INTERNATIONAL CONSIDERATIONS

Typically, organisations are founded to operate locally and then expand at some future point. First of all, this is usually a purely domestic expansion but at some point, perhaps quite soon, they will start to operate internationally. There are several steps in this process and many organisations will stop long before reaching step 4:

1. A domestic structure plus an export department (i.e. located domestically but selling internationally).
2. A domestic structure plus a foreign subsidiary or an agent.

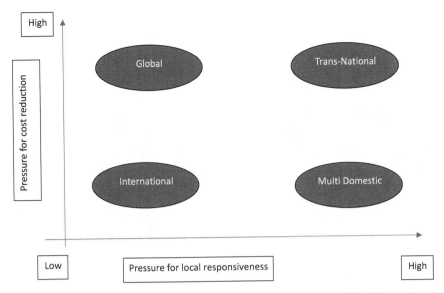

Figure 6.7 Contingent international organisational types after Bartlett and Ghoshal 1989.

3. An international division managing several export units, foreign subsidiaries and agents.
4. An international structure integrating all parts of the organisation which may be a global functional structure or a global product structure or a global geographic structure.

There have been extensive studies of the organisational designs adopted by major commercial international organisations. Bartlett and Ghoshal[7] proposed (see Figure 6.7) that the design choice depends ultimately on the balance, in each industry or sector, between the need to be responsive to local requirements (e.g. around tastes or culture) and the need to be responsive to high levels of global competition driving a need for operating costs reduction (e.g. in the automotive sector).

These contingencies lead to the idea that there are four basic types of international organisation each representing a particular strategic stance responding to those contingencies.

International organisations are highly centralised, effectively they export to their international customers what has worked well domestically. However, these organisations might be slow to react to changes in the local markets as the control is retained, more or less distantly in time, space and culture, centrally by the parent. In particular for international organisations:

- They depend only on parent company knowledge/expertise.
- The parent retains all influence and control.
- Products are developed centrally albeit sometimes minimally customised for local markets.
- All core competences are retained centrally.

Global Organisations are structured as global rather than local entities, in effect they are no longer an organisation from a particular country and even their HQ may no longer be in the original home country (indeed in these days of virtual teams it may have no physical existence at all). In particular:

- They focus on the need for global efficiency with a centralised HQ function.
- Their production is concentrated in few highly efficient factories located in whichever country offers best cost efficiency.
- They view the world as a single marketplace in which all customers are the same regardless of nationality and standardised product/ services are sold worldwide. However, regulatory requirements might be different in different markets and this might force them to make adaptations to their products and services.

Multidomestic Organisations seek to replicate the success of home country operations around the world operating locally in whatever way fits the location. In particular:

- There is a high level of delegation of authority to the local organisations.
- Their resources are localised with each subsidiary focused on a specific domestic market.
- Their products are developed for the local markets.
- Customers in each location will often have a strong perception that they are dealing with a 'local' company. However, as a consequence, there is a high potential for poor coordination.

Transnational Organisations seek to combine the benefits of global and multi domestic organisation. In particular

- They focus on dynamic strategic competencies offering, global competitiveness, multinational flexibility and worldwide knowledge management and learning capability.
- In this way, at the same time they seek, local responsiveness, global scale efficiencies and knowledge and competencies shared. But, they have many reporting lines and very complex internal communications and are quite likely to prove to be very expensive.

REBECCA RAWNSLEY – A MODERN MANAGEMENT CAREER

Q Have you been involved in the design or redesign of the structure of an organisation in your career?

I have had it done to me many times and I think that experience helped inform me in my management style and approach. I saw that engagement of the people that do the day-to-day work is often missed in the process of organisational change. Assumptions are made, observations are not made or are incorrect. For example, people are asked questions about the current structure, that is if any are asked at all, based on their title rather than on how the structure actually works. When people are ignored, they then feel quite put out, undervalued. People have lots of ideas about how to improve things. This would be a much better place to start than paying an extortionate amount for one of the big four consultancy firms. That approach is just not productive, and it can really impact the success of the organisation, which always lies in the people and their people's motivation.

Q OK, let us be specific. How can redesign of the organisation, restructuring of the organisation, be made to work so that the new organisation that appears after the process does respond to the new circumstances or strategy.

I am trying to think now if I have ever seen redesign in line with the new strategy. Have they just been a lot of redesign, upheaval, and chaos, but still not really reflecting anything of what was needed? I think Company E was maybe one of the best examples I have experienced for what should happen. Company E realised it was evolving, it was starting to bring in new expertise from different functional areas it brought in legal, mergers and acquisitions people and me as Head of Bids. That, I think was a good example of where they had figured out that they were evolving, they were growing and the impact this would have. They were no longer just the single owner venture, now they had to deliver growth because they were now private equity backed. They had figured out some core markets they wanted to focus on. Yes, I think that's probably the closest I have ever seen.

Q So that was a real strategy driven redesign and redevelopment of the organisation?

Because of its growth and the need for continuing growth they needed more public sector tender wins, bigger volumes, and values. Also, they allowed each of us to work together to come up with our own improvements. We each asked what was needed from our function and how we could work together to achieve it.

Q Achieve it as a team; that sounds like quite a sound process?

Yes, on reflection I am quite shocked it was at Company E. Interesting. Now, why would we not have had the same experience at massive international corporations like Company G and Company D? I think maybe it is because the bigger you get, the more layers there are for messages to filter through, it almost becomes no more than Chinese whispers. These organisations are huge and complicated and realistically, you cannot have a general all hands call that communicates to everybody. I think that is why the message gets diluted, confused, and twisted. So, nobody actually has that much trust or faith or commitment to it so everyone just carries on with their own plans.

Q So that comparison between the Company E example and the others is quite interesting because Company E was a small company which had suddenly recognised that it had grown and because of its new ownership, it was being forced to think its way through that process. Perhaps these other organisations may have gone through that process 50 years or more in the past.

Yes, and now they are set in their ways and I think also complacent to an extent that if you think around the big players in any market and especially in these types of markets which tend towards oligopoly. The customer's work tends to be spread around, it's one for you, one for you, one for you, and so on. Whereas the world of Company E is a lot scrappier.

Q OK, so in your experience when you are involved with these big enterprise management companies like Company G and Company F and a few others, it's an oligarchy. It's a few big players, whereas with Company E, this was red in tooth and claw. That creates a very different atmosphere at the top of the organisation. Did it create a different atmosphere at working level as well?

I think at Company E, which was still relatively small, where they did struggle with the change was that they had not embedded all the way down all of their new processes. So, there were still some of the old family run processes in place and people trying to play catch up. There was a lot of stress and pressure, but on the other hand there was still a clear view at all levels that they knew what they were, what they were trying to do. Everyone knew which key customers they were going after. There was general awareness and understanding and interaction. I think the larger the organisation it becomes the more organisational silos you get and the growth of a "you don't need to know" attitude.

Q There's some work by an academic called Richard Daft talks about the life cycle of organisations from birth through to decrepit old age, and I suspect Company G might be quite close to that latter?

Yes. At what point does the business become inefficient? What is the tipping point? At that point it has just outgrown without keeping up in some sense. Everything is held together by just a sheer hodge-podge of processes; it just about works somehow. You tend to get a lot of sticking plaster, a lot of systems with excessive complexity.

Q I call that a Baroque organisation. Any views on how to identify this tipping point?

I think it depends on the sector. Different sectors grow and expand and change more quickly, and it can also be influenced greatly by the economy. Company G has been around for 40 years, perhaps that is approaching decrepitude, on the other hand, Shell for example, has been around for far longer. Also, looking back at Company G, around 10 years ago, it rebuilt its cloud to make sure it was not just a hodgepodge that had simply grown in the ways I was just describing. That was a positive step and I wonder if now, maybe we are still in catch up. Yes, and Company E had to catch up too but in a much smaller way really.

THE CHAPTER EXAMPLE CASE – MEL

As Sarah's thinking developed, she realised that a redesign of the MEL organisational structure was going to be an important part of the plan to implement the new strategy. The current structure was functional, and this seemed still to be broadly appropriate for a smaller business making a limited range of products for a rather narrow range of customers (Figure 6.8).

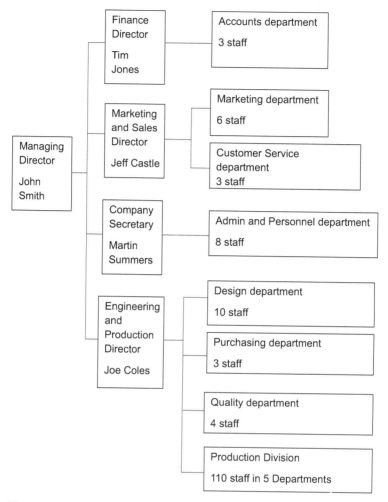

Figure 6.8 The MEL organisation structure.

Sarah's planning had identified three key areas in which organisational redesign was necessary. These were incorporated into a new organisational design shown in Figure 6.9.

- The new strategy called for the development of significant new markets in both the motorsport and energy sectors. This process of business development was a specialist task which would need to have some effort devoted directly to it. A business development specialist with experience in the proposed new markets would need to be recruited.
- The new strategy called also for a rebuilding of MEL's reputation among existing customers. To this end it was necessary to promote

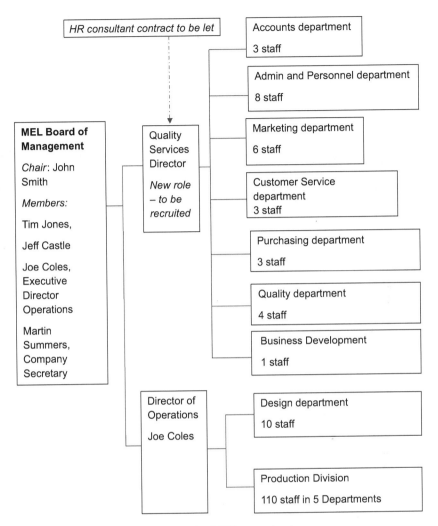

Figure 6.9 Proposed revision to the MEL organisation structure.

the visibility and role of quality in general and the quality team in particular in the culture of MEL.

- The strategy called also for steps to tackle the management team and staff age structure and groupthink concerns at MEL. Sarah's thinking on this included bringing in some new management thinking via creation of a new senior role and involving an HR consultant to identify younger recruits to bring on board in advance of the retirement of older staff as well as to create a rewards structure that linked rewards to metrics measuring performance in different parts of the organisation. Noting that quality provision to customers required that all aspects of the firm maintained quality performance, the new role would be positioned as explicitly concerned with the overall quality nature of MEL, giving it the title of Head of Quality Services. It would report to the management team now reconstituted as the Board of Management of MEL. The Operations and Design departments would continue to report to Joe Coles who would now be an Executive Director, i.e. a member of the Board with an operational role.

CHAPTER CASE – CITIGROUP CONDUCTS A MAJOR RESTRUCTURING EXERCISE

In September 2023, Citigroup announced large changes to its structure. The guiding principle was to reorient the bank, which had long been known for its geographic reach, around its lines of business rather than where it operated. The reorganisation, when complete, would wipe out five layers of management, cutting them down to eight from 13. It was intended to fully align its management structure with its new business strategy and overall, to simplify the bank. There would be a shift from having two large business units – one focused on commercial clients and the other on its consumer businesses – to five divisions made up of its primary business segments. The heads of those five units would report directly to the CEO, eliminating a previous layer of management between the chief executive and the business heads. It would also allow these five business leaders to have greater influence on Citi's strategy and its execution, while enhancing accountability.

In addition, Leadership of the firm's geographies outside of North America was to be consolidated under a new Head of International, instead of having multiple regional heads. The scope of the local geographic management would be narrowed to focus solely on local clients. While a newly created global client organisation would be responsible for strengthening client engagement and experience across the bank's global network and businesses.

The new flatter structure would ultimately eliminate several management layers, to speed up decision making and strengthen the focus on clients. A press release quoted the CEO as saying this.

> I am determined that our bank will deliver to our full potential, and we're making bold decisions to meet our commitments to all our stakeholders. These changes eliminate unnecessary complexity across the bank, increase accountability for delivering excellent

client service and strengthen our ability to benefit from the natural linkages that exist amongst our businesses, all with an eye toward delivering on our medium-term targets.........

The press release emphasised that while not exiting any of the countries it operated in, and that there remained commitment to the bank's international focus as a critical differentiator from rivals. Nevertheless, the CEO said that eliminating much of Citi's geographic management was a big part of where the bank could cut costs and simplify.

> "When we formed our regional organisation many, many years ago, it was a very different bank," the CEO said at an investor conference shortly after announcing the reorganisation. "We just don't need that type of heavy management structure and local governance and processes."

Financial reporters at the time said that the changes came as the CEO battled to turn around the third-largest US bank by assets, which for years had lagged peers and been dogged by operational and regulatory issues. They quoted the CEO as saying that the reorganisation would "eliminate needless complexity" but acknowledging it would result in "saying goodbye to some very talented and hard-working colleagues". It was also reported that, internally, some Citi employees were enthusiastic for the CEO's renewed efforts to re-energise and streamline the bank, which some complained was too bogged down by bureaucracy. An employee is quoted as saying this.

> There was lots of logic to what she was doing, because we were just running too much cost in this business.

Banking commentators report one Citigroup manager as remarking that Citi had often become mired in a matrix of overlapping leadership so that any decision that needed to be made had to get approved by three bosses. The CEO emphasised that the restructuring was about improving the operations and efficiency of the bank, which many said had long been plagued by its "matrix" management structure, and not purely about cost-cutting. Citi hoped the restructuring would revive its stock price, which had been the sector's worst performer, and improve the bank's lagging returns.

It was reported that Citigroup expected to cut at least 20,000 jobs, about 10% of its workforce, costing as much as $1.8bn but saving as much as $2.5bn a year by 2026 when the restructuring was due to be completed. On top of the jobs cut through the restructuring process, the bank expected to shed another 40,000 workers through planned exiting from its consumer banking business in Mexico and elsewhere.

CASE DISCUSSION QUESTIONS

1. Research the performance of Citigroup in 2024 and the views of financial analysts on the outcome from the restructuring described here. Was the idea and its implementation a success?
2. Use the ideas advanced in this chapter to analyse the Citi changes.

CLASS DISCUSSION QUESTIONS

1. Explain the relationship between design of the organisation and its strategic context.
2. It might be said that centralisation is key to ensuring control and that organisations do, and do well, what they have been set up to do. What are your comments on this point of view?
3. Why is the age of an organisation relevant to its performance?
4. Can there be too little internal conflict in an organisation?
5. Identify examples of each of the Bartlett and Ghoshal organisational types.

CHAPTER SUMMARY

- There is no best way to design an organisation. Everything depends on the context, on the environment, on the market, on the technology and on the history of the organisation and previous decisions.
- A good organisational structure will enable action to deliver the organisational mission, will reduce transaction costs and will be able flexibly to respond to changing circumstances.
- A bad organisation typically displays slow and inadequate decision making, fails to be innovative and exhibits excess internal conflict.

- There is always an informal organisation as well as the formal one set out in organisation charts and similar ways. It is looser and more flexible and more spontaneous but nonetheless very powerful as it meets the personal needs of people. Successful managers will be fully aware of the informal organisation around their employees and will be fully part of their own informal groups and relationships, often extending outside the organisation.
- Formal organisational structures can be categorised into three main types: the unitary or functional structure, the divisional structure, and the matrix structure.
- International commercial organisations tend to fall into one of four organisational types, international, global, multidomestic and transnational depending on the need for cost efficiency and the need for local responsiveness in their sector.

NOTES

1 Burns, T. and Stalker, G.M. (2004) *Mechanistic and Organic Systems*, London: Routledge.
2 Mintzberg, H. (1979) *The Structuring of Organizations*, Upper Saddle River, NJ: Prentice Hall.
3 Daft, R.L. (2008) *Organisation Theory and Design*, Boston, MA: South-Western Cengage.
4 Williamson, O.E. (2008) outsourcing, transaction cost economics and supply chain management. *Journal of Supply Chain Management*, 44(2): 2–82.
5 Galbraith, J.R. and Kates, A. (2007) *Designing your Organisation*, Hoboken, NJ: Wiley.
6 Teece, D.J., Pisano, G., and Shuen, A. (1997) Dynamic capabilities and strategic management. *Strategic Management Journal*, 18.
7 Bartlett, C. and Ghoshal, S. (1989) Managing across borders: The transnational solution. *Academy of Management Review*. Valhalla, NY.

7 Emergent Properties of Organisations: Culture, Power, and Politics

SETTING THE SCENE

It was pointed out earlier that organisations are human societies and therefore, will exhibit all the characteristics of society in general. These will always exist and they include organisational culture; the use and abuse of organisational internal power and the political behaviour used to acquire and deploy power within the organisation.

Organisational culture might be thought of as the personality of an organisation. It decides how things are done in an organisation, daily. It affects how employees perform their work; how they relate to each other; to their customers and to their managers. Managers are of course, themselves part of that culture but it is crucial that they are aware of this and can understand how best to manage in this specific context. Equally, it will be seen that the effective manager will need to be aware of the potential sources of power within the organisation and to develop the skills and relationships to be able to acquire and use that power. This will be particularly important at times of change and doubt about organisational direction and, often, changing the organisational culture will be an important part of responding to these times of change.

It is important also to note that this culture is made up of many elements. It includes the personal culture of many individuals each of whom will have their own history and experience, both individual and organisational, as well as a national culture, and perhaps a distinct professional culture (e.g. consider the differences between the culture of the nursing team and that of the sales team). Thus, the culture of the organisation is built up in levels from individual through team to suborganisation, to overall organisation. Indeed, one may also consider how the organisation as a whole is part of a particular industry or sectoral culture.

DOI: 10.4324/9781032686592-7

NATIONAL CULTURE

The fundamental building block of the organisation is the individual, so we start there with a consideration of national culture.

As we have already noted, organisational cultures are not independent from the cultural milieu which surround and intersect them. Principal among these is the question of national culture. It is a subject which has been studied extensively and has proved important in helping people to understand what to expect when moving abroad to work in another country or when thinking about setting up business operations or starting to do business with customers and partners and other stakeholders in other countries.

The most referenced ideas are those of Geert Hofstede[1] who conducted his initial studies in the late 1960s focusing on the employees of IBM which then had more than 100,000 people spread over 60 countries. There is a reasonable criticism of Hofstede's work that it is increasingly out of date in the modern globalised world but equally, the very concept of globalisation might well be challenged. There are other substantive criticisms too, but the most important point is to avoid stereotyping the individuals and groups we meet. Work such as Hofstede's only applies to very large groups of people, national cultures taken as a whole, and certainly does not necessarily apply to any individual.

Based on his studies of varying cultural predispositions Hofstede proposed a model of national culture consisting of four dimensions.

- **Power Distance** – The level of acceptance by a society of the unequal distribution of power in institutions. For example, if this is low superiors are accessible and if high, they are inaccessible.
- **Uncertainty Avoidance** – The extent to which people in a society feel threatened by ambiguous situations. For example, if low then there should be as few rules as possible and if high there is a great felt need for detailed written rules and procedures.
- **Individualism** – The tendency of people to look after themselves and their immediate families only and to neglect the needs of society; identity is based on the individual.
- **Collectivism** – The desire for tight social frameworks, feeling emotional dependence on belonging to "the organisation", and a strong belief in group decisions, identity is based on the social system.
- **Masculinity** – The degree to which traditionally masculine values (e.g. assertiveness, materialism, and lack of concern for others) prevail in the society.

- **Femininity** – the degree to which caring values prevail. For example, around quality of life as opposed to emphasising high levels of performance.

By considering each of these dimensions, we can see what is likely to be the result if an organisation based around one national culture simply reproduces itself to operate with a different national culture:

- Get the power distance wrong and people can feel snubbed or exposed.
- Get the uncertainty avoidance wrong and people can feel oppressed or anxious.
- Get the individualism/collectivism wrong and people can feel suffocated or abandoned.
- Get the masculinity/femininity wrong and people can feel demotivated or overwhelmed by pressure of work.

The figure[2] below indicates the results found for a variety of countries (Figure 7.1).

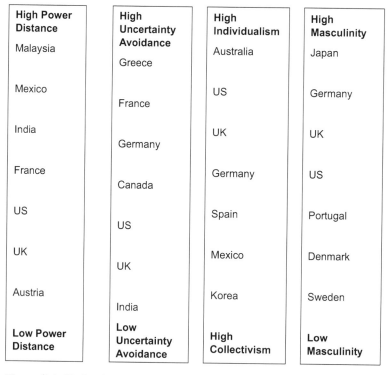

High Power Distance	High Uncertainty Avoidance	High Individualism	High Masculinity
Malaysia	Greece	Australia	Japan
Mexico	France	US	Germany
India	Germany	UK	UK
France	Canada	Germany	US
US	US	Spain	Portugal
UK	UK	Mexico	Denmark
Austria	India	Korea	Sweden
Low Power Distance	**Low Uncertainty Avoidance**	**High Collectivism**	**Low Masculinity**

Figure 7.1 Hofstede's Dimensions – results for various countries adapted from Deresky (2023).

Another very useful approach is that of Edward Hall[3] who looked explicitly at differences in communication and in attitudes towards time. Whilst not empirically established his models have proved to be useful in developing an understanding of how differences in approach in different national cultures can lead to misunderstanding and how this might be avoided.

Hall refers to cultures as falling on a spectrum between being High Context and Low Context. The term "context" refers to the extent to which all aspects of the surroundings and situation, e.g. the physical or social situation and body language, around a message are as important as the message itself. This can be high or low so that individuals from high or low context cultures have different ways of communicating and hence of experiencing the world. In high-context cultures information is pre-programmed within the individual receiver of the message and the context. Only minimal information is transmitted in the message. Messaging is subtle, indirect, and hidden, e.g. a request is declined with vagueness or body language. In a low-context culture the messaging is overt, frank and to the point and so a request is declined by saying "no" (Figure 7.2).

Hall refers also to cultures as tending to be Polychronic or Monochronic. He called this Time Orientation.

- Monochronic – usually focusing on one task at a time, with a strong preference for completing tasks in a timely fashion, schedule driven, deadline focused.
- Polychronic – usually willing to juggle many tasks at once, happy to be interrupted from the current task, not driven by deadlines.

It will be evident how easily misunderstandings, mistakes and breakdowns in relationships can occur in the light of different approaches to communication and different attitudes to time identified by Hall.

ORGANISATIONAL CULTURE

It should be acknowledged immediately that the idea of the existence of a culture unique to an organisation remains somewhat controversial. In general, it is recognised that organisations have "something" (a personality, philosophy, ideology, or climate) which goes beyond economic rationality, and which gives each of them a unique identity. Moving beyond this, the specific concept called organisational culture has been variously described as "the way we do things around here",[4] "how people behave when no one is watching", and "the collective programming of the mind" (Hofstede, 2001). In this book, I take the view that the key point to recognise is that an organisation is a society, it is a human

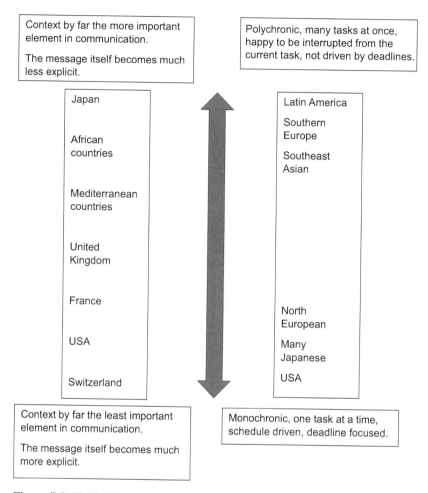

Figure 7.2 Hall's High and Low Context and Time Orientation – Some national results. Adapted from Hall and Hall, 1987.

community albeit formed for a special purpose and that over time it will develop its own separate culture just like any other community.

Organisational culture is defined in various ways. A practical approach is offered by Buchanan and Huczynski.[5]

> The collection of relatively uniform and enduring values, beliefs, customs, traditions and practices that are shared by an organisation's members, learned by new recruits, and transmitted from one generation of employees to the next.

But we should recognise that organisations are open systems which include people coming from other organisations, having varying professions, which likely include people from different sociocultural backgrounds, and which are affected by the context in which they operate. All these different cultural levels operate simultaneously to make up the overall cultural background of an organisation.

One might perhaps think of organisational culture as the personality of that collective entity which is an organisation. It affects how employees perform their work; how they relate to each other; to customers and to their managers. But it does not only impact task issues, it influences also how well or badly an organisation performs and how workers feel about their work and their company. It deals with how things are done in a company day to day without any especial thought or decision-making process. Thus Ann Cunliffe[6] states that organisational culture is important because it:

- shapes the image that the public has of an organisation.
- influences organisational effectiveness.
- provides direction for the company.
- helps to attract, retain, and motivate staff.

It is possible also to characterise organisational culture as existing on a spectrum from Strong to Weak. If it is strong then organisation members have a strong emotional attachment to the values of the organisations, this set of values is very widespread across the organisation and largely unchallenged and the members will show evident approval or disapproval of the actions and views of others assessed against these values. A weak culture, by contrast, is one in which there is little agreement among employees about their organisation's core values. A strong culture is thought to act to unite staff and direct their attitudes and actions, but this does not necessarily make it a good culture. Employees might hold inappropriate attitudes and managers may make wrong decisions especially as times change. A strong culture will have developed over a considerable period and inevitably incorporates much learned behaviour which may no longer be appropriate. A strong culture may also impede success if it encourages conformist attitudes and causes inertia and a lack of creativity and innovation.

The strength of a culture depends on the similarity of its employees, and the length and intensity of their shared experiences within the firm. An important part of this is the process of socialisation during which an employee's pattern of behaviour, values, attitudes, and motives is influenced in a direction to conform to those of the organisation. This includes the careful selection of new company members, instruction in appropriate ways of thinking and behaving, and the reinforcement of desired behaviours by senior managers. Of course, this should remind us of the processes by which groupthink takes root and grows, perhaps to a dangerous degree. Colquitt[7] gives a list of pros and cons for strong cultures:

Pro

- Differentiates the organisation from others.
- Allows employees to identify themselves with the organisation.
- Facilitates behaviour desired by management, among employees.
- Creates stability within the organisation.

Con

- Makes merging with another organisation more difficult.
- Attracts and retains similar kinds of employees thereby limiting the diversity of thought, creativity, and innovation.
- Can create extreme behaviours among employees.
- Makes adapting to the changing environment more difficult.

Clearly the culture of an organisation is a very important factor in the performance of the organisation. To this end it is useful to be able to characterise different types of culture, beyond just whether they are strong or weak as a basis for considering how the culture might need to change in line with changing circumstances. A very influential book by Charles Handy[8] identifies four basic types of organisational culture.

- **Power** cultures have a single, dominant individual who exerts their will; controlling by recruiting those of a similar viewpoint; and operating with the minimum of rules. Decisions are based on maintenance of the balance of power rather than logic, and there is little emphasis on discussion to reach consensus. An example is a small company run by its founder or individual owner.
- **Role** culture is bureaucratic emphasising the importance of rules and operating procedures. Managers operate "by the book", in line with their position in the hierarchy and their role. It is structured around functional departments and specialties, and its operations are driven by logic and rationality. A typical example would be a government department or a university administration.
- **Person** cultures are focused on individuals. They exist for the benefit of their members, and control is exercised only by mutual consent so that the organisation is seen as subordinates to the individuals. This type of culture is typical of professional partnerships such architects, design teams etc.

- **Task** cultures are job or project oriented. The task is specified at the top, but then the emphasis shifts to finding the resources, and then getting the job done through using individuals' enthusiasm and commitment, working as a team. Influence within this culture is based on the expert, rather than position or personal status. Such cultures are found in client-focused agencies such as advertising companies or management consultancies.

Another approach would be to have a way to model or map the specific organisational culture of an organisation so that one could then, e.g., compare it with others or plan what it should look like if it were to be better performing in changed circumstances. We could then plan a change process to move towards that new organisational culture (see Chapter 9). Such a tool is the idea of constructing a cultural web of an organisation which was originally proposed by Johnson and Scholes[9] and which shows how the organisational culture manifests in behaviours, symbols and physical aspects of the organisation. The important point here is that these are things we can observe and record as a basis for understanding the culture. Johnson and Scholes suggest that these observable aspects of culture fall into the following set of overlapping and interacting categories.

- Stories – told to outsiders and new recruits and serving to embed organisational history and indicate conventional norms.
- Symbols – refer to anything, from objects to language, that carries meaning beyond its functional purpose. For example, as a junior civil servant I was in a large, shared office with a linoleum floor and just a room number on the door but after promotion to the next rank, I shared with only one other person of the same rank, and we had our names and positions on the door and pieces of carpet to go under our feet. These symbols confirmed our status and reinforced the hierarchy.
- Power structures – are about the reality of power distribution in the organisation as opposed to the theoretical organisational structure. Those holding significant power will be very influential in maintaining, controlling, regulating and reinforcing the cultural paradigm, representing the established way of doing things.
- Organisational structures – are the formally stated reporting relationships and responsibilities that describe how the organisational tasks are delivered in terms of action and accountability and control. They will often be very similar to the power structures, but they are not the same as power can pass

through informal relationships. Organisational structures, as power structures, reflect the history of long-established organisations.

- Control systems – the formal and informal mechanisms to monitor and support people in the organisation which tend to emphasise whatever is seen as being important in the organisation. For example, individual bonus schemes tend to signal a culture of competition rather than one of teamwork.
- Routines and rituals – are the day-to-day repeated processes and activities which are taken for granted as the normal content of daily organisational life. They are not thought about, they just happen. They are difficult to change and reflect the history of long-established organisations.
- Paradigm – that set of assumptions commonly held and taken for granted within the organisation. As such they are not evident to members of the organisation and hence can be very difficult to change. The paradigm assumptions influence the other aspects of the cultural web and the paradigm is then reinforced by those other elements so that the culture builds and strengthens itself over time.

POWER AND POLITICS

Organisations are political systems; politics is the art of leading a human community and that is exactly what an organisation is. Thus, Organisational Politics is defined by Buchanan and Huczynski[10] as

> those activities undertaken within an organisation to acquire, develop and use power and other resources to obtain one's preferred outcomes in a situation in which there is uncertainty or an absence of consensus about choices.

As a manager it is essential to manage politics and deploy power effectively. Just because a manager does not take an interest in politics doesn't mean politics won't take an interest in the manager (to misquote Pericles of Athens).

Box 7.1 Adapted from Wikipedia Accessed on 20/03/2024

Pericles (495–429 BCE) was a Greek politician and general during the Golden Age of Athens. He was prominent and influential in Ancient Athenian politics, particularly between the Greco-Persian Wars and the Peloponnesian War.

Indeed, to ignore politics practically ensures that the manager will lose effectiveness due to losing out in the acquisition of organisational power. Such a manager, at the least, will be letting down their own teams. Managers who do not have power, and who are either unwilling or unable to use the politics of their organisations, have difficulty in getting anything done.

Often, we mistakenly think that human behaviour is based on logic and that decision making is rational and supports clear goals. Whereas communications actually are not open and power, and conflict does really influence decision making. Further organisations comprise individuals and coalitions with divergent goals and interests and information is unevenly available. All decision making is thus influenced by differences in power, and it is often not wholly or even partly rational. Daft[11] (1992) can help us in understanding the power and politics relationships in an organisation by identifying when it is likely to be most prominent:

- At times of structural change in the organisation, we see the use of political activities to better position a group or individual in the new organisation and to grow in power for that future.
- In processes of interdepartmental coordination which inevitably involve the relative power and influence or different groups and individuals.
- When resources are being allocated, because these are a key source of power and influence giving the group capability to do what it does more and to become more central in the overall organisational functioning.
- At times of management succession as the role available will be a direct source of enhanced power and influence.

This is reflected in some work done by Pfeffer and quoted by Buchanan and Huczynski.[12] Pfeffer argues that management failures can often be attributed to failings in political skills. Power can be defined as the ability to get other people to do what you want them to do, and it is often necessary to use political tactics to achieve those ends; politics might be thought of as power in action. Pfeffer offers the following list of sources of power:

- Formal position and authority offer a legitimate power to direct.
- Ability to cultivate allies and supporters creates a powerbase.
- Access and control over information and resources gives power over the ability of others to achieve.
- Physical and social position confers status.

- Centrality of own unit in the organisation structure makes a person indispensable to others.
- Role of resolving critical problems makes a person indispensable to others.
- Degree of unity/lack of dissent in the organisation contributes to the power of those at the head of that unity.
- Being irreplaceable to other members of the organisation.
- Organisational pervasiveness of one's activities.

Organisational change especially at times of great dynamism in the external environment, creates many unstructured decisions points, particularly about the direction and purpose of change, and also how the goals of change should best be achieved. The scope for political behaviour during periods of major change is therefore high. Change also generates uncertainty, and those who have the appropriate political knowledge and skill can exploit that uncertainty to their advantage, to influence decisions in their preferred direction, and to position themselves favourably in the new structure.

Beeman and Sharkey[13] addressed the question of how excessive political behaviour in organisations might be addressed. Their work produced three guiding principles:

1. Reduce system uncertainty:

   a. Make sure it is clear to all what are the bases and processes for evaluation.
   b. Differentiate rewards to create real differences between low and high performers.
   c. Make sure the rewards are as directly related to performance as possible.

2. Reduce Competition, likely requiring review of targets and performance indicators:

   a. Try to minimise resource competition among managers.
   b. Replace internal resource competition with externally oriented goals and objectives.

3. Break up existing political fiefdoms:

   a. Split dysfunctional sub-groups.

We shall be returning to the management of change and the role in this of power and politics in Chapter 9.

REBECCA RAWNSLEY – A MODERN MANAGEMENT CAREER

Q I think that organisational culture is often at the root of organisational success and even more of organisational failure. I wonder whether that is aligned with your own experience?

Yeah, I would say it is. It is the organisational culture that drives how people are feeling, how they feel valued or not.

Q How do you think that new people discover organisational culture, how do they accommodate to it?

I think it would depend at what level they are joining an organisation, and it depends also on the individual. It depends on your ability to read between the lines. But the process required is to speak to your colleagues in the team, gaining their trust so that then they start speaking freely. They will let you know about the people who are important. Who calls the shots. If you come in a little more senior it is still about observation, but I think the onus is more on you to be able to determine for yourself how things work because you're maybe less able to go and ask more junior people. At a more junior level it is normal for you to go to chat to your teammates. When you join at a senior level, there's more expectations on you immediately from the more junior people. It is through building trust that I have I always learnt a lot from my team however, because I cannot see everything that goes on; I deal with different countries, time zones and locations. So, getting to know the culture is about socialising and I think it is emotional intelligence that makes the difference.

Q Do you think people make day-to-day decisions purely based on the culture?

Yes, I think they do, You have it at the back of your mind. Who is it that you're speaking to and what is important to them? However, that doesn't necessarily mean it's the organisation strategy that you're aligning to. Or the best interests of the organisation. Inevitably you are being steered in a particular direction because you need to pitch. You need to sell your ideas to get buy in from certain people. There is also the question of where power lies and the individual viewpoints of the powerful. People consider their own personal goals that may not be in the business best interests, that is their individual goals, whether they are translated from the organisation goals or whether there is more of a personal agenda involved.

Q Do you think that organisational culture extends into business decision making so that there are norms and expectations of what this business will want to do, and therefore what I ought to decide?

Certainly, yes. For example, sales; if there is a desire for a certain type of customer then obviously throughout all the areas of business it will be decided to go for those customers. Of course, it might not necessarily be worth the investment. But the salesperson knows it will impress senior people so yes, we need to go for it, even if we are unlikely to be successful, we need to show willing. I think it also applies with any kind of changes of process, if we know that there could be upset because it goes against norms and the views of those in power. All of this may be for the best, but it may not. It may be comfortable, but it may not enhance efficiency or revenue.

Q An example might be chasing market share by cutting prices?

Yes, I have often seen that. For example it is often the case that my companies wanted public sector customers, the view was that public sector was where the big money was, that it was huge. True, but not all of it is big. Do you want that small local government contract of only £50,000? Perhaps no but they felt the need to go for it, to go after these customers based on a vague and generic definition of a customer type.

Q I think clarity is a key point there, isn't it, because it seems to me that one of the things about the culture is that it gives artificial clarity, makes decisions easy?

Yes, because vague statements are often the way that organisations go. Because of that lack of clarity each team, each department, everyone could go in different ways. So, that interpretation, that local clarification, will always conform to what is seen as the historical norm and so it just goes on into the future.

Q Yes, it is natural to do what you are comfortable with and know you can do?

Yes, protect yourself reduce the risk to yourself and reduce the amount of thinking you must do. So, changing organisational culture is probably the hardest thing of all to change. For example, all software vendors know that they need to be more customer oriented rather than technically, product oriented. But that is the historical norm, the way in which the industry was built and became very successful. But that hasn't necessarily been communicated very well. The words are there in every slide deck but how is it being addressed from the point of view of the cultural shift that is needed? There is now a bit of a power balance fight between that the old view and the new. The historical norms are not being addressed clearly instead everyone is bickering and many people are being very cautious about toeing the party line. Whichever party line is represented by their team leader. But, talking to them privately, you often see they have a very different view.

Q I found in a previous job of mine that these sorts of communication problems were exacerbated by the fact that we were a dispersed organisation internationally and even around the UK with many locations. Is that the same with Company G that?

I don't think so, it is not necessarily the case because Company G, and Company F, were pretty much always spread across the globe and a common, rather strong, organisational culture emerged. But of course, national cultural differences continue to exist. My colleagues in the Middle East are fantastic at their jobs but they are very comfortable working in a rather chaotic way which sometimes, I can find difficult, and our internal processes can find challenging. But then, it is the norm for their customers!

Q So, this can lead to a breakdown in understanding and internal communications.

Yes, but obviously they have the local knowledge and that's why they are so important. We need the local cultural feel to be able to respond appropriately to our customers. But this does conflict with the central pressure to be "one Company G". Not to be separate lines of business. All to be on message.

THE CHAPTER EXAMPLE CASE – MEL

The strategy which Sarah was seeking to implement required that the organisational culture be improved in relation to its attitude to quality in general and performance to customer specification in particular.

This new culture would be one of the bases for MEL being again recognised as the best-in-class provider in all its markets.

Sarah recalled that the management team attributed their initial and continuing success to their values as innovative engineers, expressed in the company mission "keeping up to date keeps us well ahead of the rest". There were well-established systems intended to ensure continuous improvement as part of a first-class Total Quality Management (TQM) system. In the past and up to relatively recently, an innovative approach to manufacturing systems as well as to products had allowed MEL successfully to grow, despite the highly competitive nature of all their markets.

What had gone wrong? Talking to Adam, one of her team of change agents who was a member of the quality team, she learned that he felt that the quality team was demotivated (see Chapter 4). But he also said that, in comparison with his previous experience, he had observed that the MEL implementation of TQM had become a tick box exercise rather than reflecting real assessment of quality performance. A fundamental problem, given the nature of the customers and the competitiveness of the motorsport sector, was that the idea of continuous improvement was no longer at the forefront of people's minds. The concept had become a mere symbol rather than an active process. Adam put this down to a more general feeling of demotivation, or perhaps tiredness, across the organisation that seemed to him to affect people at every level. Adam told Sarah that the MEL quality culture needed urgently to be revived and relaunched.

Sarah knew that this sort of culture change would not follow from some sort of management edict. Rather she needed to create an internal movement that would spread recognition of the need for new attitudes and values around every aspect of the activities at MEL. Sarah also knew that such a movement would emerge only if it was initiated and demonstrated in actions rather than words from the top of the organisation.

- Her proposed organisational changes would be an important part of this. They would demonstrate that the current management team was prepared to step back from day-to-day control and especially, the creation of a new Head of Quality Services post would reinforce this.
- But it would be important also to take some immediate operational steps, around key customer's work, that would show that MEL was conscious of the concerns being felt by customers and was prepared to tackle the underlying problems head on. The Executive Director for Operations would need to lead on this in person.

- Investment in the new senior management role and remedial recruitment of new staff to learn from older staff before they retired would also demonstrate clear management intent that MEL should and must, now change.

It was also obvious to Sarah, from her thinking about the whole process of change management that to have impact and for that impact to be sustained beyond the short term, this culture movement would need to be driven by a clear and spreading acceptance that change was absolutely necessary (see Chapter 9).

CHAPTER CASE: TRANSFORMATION AT ROLLS-ROYCE

In March 2023 Rolls-Royce announced changes to its Board and Executive Team, saying that they were adding leaders with proven track records of delivering success and a strong commitment to creating a high-performing, competitive, resilient and growing business. This followed the launch by Chief Executive Tufan Erginbilgic of a transformation programme requiring a winning culture and shared determination to deliver sustainable earnings growth and cash generation. The changes announced included the addition to senior leadership of people with extensive multinational experience in finance and performance management and with substantial industry experience in both Civil Aerospace and Defence.

- Firstly, there was to be a new Chief Financial Officer, bringing more than 25 years of experience in senior finance and performance management roles within complex multinational engineering organisations.
- The remit of the existing President – Rolls-Royce Electrical was expanded to cover all Civil Aerospace to bring a fresh perspective and energy to Civil Aerospace as the business focuses on delivering increased cash, profitability and returns. He had been with Rolls-Royce for 13 years and previously held leadership positions in Defence aerospace as well as working as Chief of Staff to the Chief Executive.
- Meanwhile the existing President Civil Aerospace became Group President taking on executive responsibility for the Group's nuclear operations including Rolls-Royce Submarines, and of Rolls-Royce SMR which has a nuclear power plant design well placed to succeed in the current selection process being organised by the UK Government.

- Finally, the existing head of Defence global service operations was appointed President – Defence, and as Chairman & CEO – Rolls-Royce North America.

Tufan Erginbilgic, Rolls-Royce Chief Executive, said: ".... [the new CFO's] .... track record of promoting rigorous financial discipline and experience of delivering performance management to achieve dramatic improvements will be invaluable as we move, at pace, to transform Rolls-Royce ...". He added:

> .... With the leadership changes announced today we are acting at pace and gaining the momentum we need to transform Rolls-Royce. Together, my leadership team has a winning mindset, strong strategic alignment, and a shared ambition to make Rolls-Royce a company that delivers for all stakeholders.

A further press release in November 2023 outlined the changes that Rolls-Royce was seeking to make in its culture and operations as follows.

Box 7.2 Taken from a Rolls-Royce Press Release November 2023

Chief Executive Tufan Erginbilgic said:

> Rolls-Royce is at a pivotal point in its history. After a strong start to our transformation programme, we are today laying out a clear vision for the journey we need to take and the areas where we must focus. We are creating a high performing, competitive, resilient, and growing Rolls-Royce that will have the financial strength to control and shape its own destiny. We are confident in our ability to achieve these ambitions and have a clear and granular plan to deliver on our targets. We have made significant progress, with 2023 profit and cash forecast to be materially ahead of 2022".
>
> We are setting compelling and achievable financial targets for the mid-term which will take Rolls-Royce significantly beyond any previous financial performance. This will benefit not just our shareholders but our people, customers and partners. We are building 'one Rolls-Royce'. A company that can fully realise its potential, ensuring the excellence and innovation that helped shape the modern world, endures long into the future.

- Clear vision and strategy will create a high performing, competitive, resilient, and growing business.
- Mid-term targets set to deliver record future performance: operating profit of £2.5bn-£2.8bn, operating margin of 13%–15%, free cashflow of £2.8bn-£3.1bn and return on Company Cl of 16%–18%.
- Improved financial performance will create a stronger balance sheet and investment grade profile for the benefit of all stakeholders.
- Focused strategy has identified investment priorities, partnership opportunities and supports a £1bn-£1.5bn gross disposal programme over next five years.
- These targets, the performance improvements that underpin them and the actions we require to achieve them, are owned across the Group and supported through rigorous performance management and clear lines of accountability.

Commenting on these developments at Rolls-Royce the Financial Times said that despite its longstanding position as Britain's pre-eminent engineer, Rolls-Royce's operating margins have historically underperformed those of larger peers such as America's General Electric. More recently, its pursuit of trying to win market share from rival engine makers saw it sometimes sacrifice profitability and price. The FT concluded that "The [newly set] ambitious profit and free cash flow targets could be taken to 'imply that Rolls-Royce is willing to shed revenues in exchange for better profitability and cash flow, if so, it is a deeper culture change from Rolls-Royce's traditional market share optimisation approach of past decades'".

When Erginbilgic took over from his predecessor he joined with a reputation as a formidable operator. He acted quickly to put his stamp on the organisation; almost half of Rolls-Royce's senior executives changed positions or left as part of the restructuring and the move to centralise core functions such as human resources and purchasing. Erginbilgic has been eager to stress a company-led turnaround rather than one that depends on the market. He said "It is our actions that are driving the performance. It is not the environment", The targets, Erginbilgic said, "actually mean a step change in performance".

Sources: Rolls-Royce press releases of march and November 2023, Financial Times articles of November 2023 and January 2024.

CASE DISCUSSION QUESTIONS

1. The FT refer to these developments as implying a culture change in Rolls-Royce. Do you agree?
2. What might be the purpose of such widespread changes in senior management?

CLASS DISCUSSION QUESTIONS

1. Hall offers two approaches to understanding national cultural differences. Outline the two approaches giving examples.
2. How does Hall's thinking on national culture differ from Hofstede's?
3. Define organisational politics. Are they a bad thing?
4. Outline Handy's model of cultural types and apply it to two contrasting cases of your choice.
5. It might be said that a strong organisational culture is essential as it ensures that all parts of the organisation act similarly. Comment on this point of view.

CHAPTER SUMMARY

*   Organisations are human societies and exhibit all the characteristics of society in general. These will always exist and include organisational culture; the use and abuse of organisational internal power and the political behaviour used to acquire and deploy power within the organisation.
*   Organisational culture is made up of the enduring values, beliefs, customs, traditions, and practices that are shared by an organisation's members and learned by new recruits. But also, organisations are open systems and people join from other organisations and varying professions, which likely include people from different sociocultural backgrounds, and which are affected by the context in which they operate.
*   National cultural differences are one of the key elements contributing to the overall organisational culture and impact

also relations with external stakeholders. Hofstede's model is useful in distinguishing between four factors contributing to national culture and providing research results of the value of these factors in different countries and regions. The four factors are power distance, Uncertainty Avoidance, Individualism and Masculinity.

- Organisational politics are those activities undertaken within an organisation to acquire, develop and use power and other resources.

NOTES

1 Hofstede, G. (1984) *Culture's Consequences: International Differences in Work-Related Values* (2nd Ed.), Beverly Hills, CA: SAGE.
2 Deresky, H. and Miller, S.R. (2023) *International Management: Managing across Borders and Cultures*, Upper Saddle River, NJ: Pearson.
3 Steers, R.M. (2016) *Management across Cultures*, Cambridge: Cambridge University Press.
4 Deal, T. and Kennedy, A. (1982) *Corporate Cultures: The Rites and Rituals of Corporate Life*, Boston, MA: Addison-Wesley.
5 Buchanan, D.A. and Huczynski, A.A. (2019) *Organizational Behaviour* (10th Ed.), Harlow: Pearson.
6 Cunliffe, A.L. (2008) *Organisation Theory*, London: Sage.
7 Colquitt, J. (2009) *Organizational Behaviour: Essentials for Improving Performance and Commitment*, New York City, NY: McGraw-Hill.
8 Handy, C.B. (1976) *Understanding Organisations*, London: Penguin Books.
9 Whittington, R., Regnér, P., Angwin, D., Johnson, G. and Scholes, K., (2020) *Exploring Strategy*, Harlow: Pearson.
10 Buchanan, D.A. and Huczynski, A.A. (2019) *Organizational Behaviour* (10th Ed.), Harlow: Pearson.
11 Daft, R.L. (1992) *Organization Theory and Design*, Eagan, MN: West Publishing Company.
12 Buchanan, D.A. and Huczynski, A.A. (2019) *Organizational Behaviour* (10th Ed.), Harlow: Pearson.
13 Beeman, D.R. and Sharkey, T.W. (1987) The use and abuse of corporate politics. *Business Horizons*, Elsevier, 30(2): 26–30.

8 Leadership

INTRODUCTION

In any group, however small it is, leadership will emerge. The search for leadership and the giving and acceptance of leadership are fundamental parts of the human condition. Northouse[1] describes leadership as the process whereby an individual influences a group of individuals to achieve a common goal.

In this chapter we shall seek to dispel several key myths about leadership such as:

- Leadership outcomes are attributable wholly to the leader, seen as the hero, the "Great Man" – in fact the real agency of leadership is through the actions of the leader's followers.
- There exists a formula for effective leadership – in fact leadership is highly dynamic and must be approached in the light of the current situation.
- The results of leadership are more important than the processes by which they are achieved – not only is this an egregious example of the moral fallacy that the ends justify the means, but it also ignores the social role of the leader. That is what they symbolise, how effectively they motivate, and what they represent to followers about the future; these are all crucial to the group.

Our favoured approach is to recognise that leadership is contingent, that it is a dynamic system which occurs in society and is the consequence of an interlocking set of factors:

DOI: 10.4324/9781032686592-8

- The context and the leader's recognition of that context.
- The leader's relationship with the followers.
- The follower's motivation and ability to deliver organisational outcomes given the context.

BACKGROUND TO LEADERSHIP THEORY

Over very many the years leadership has been conceptualised in many ways, but four components can be identified as central:

1. It is a process of direction, connecting mission to outcomes.
2. It involves influencing other people.
3. It occurs in groups of all sizes.
4. It involves delivery of common goals.

Box 8.1

A broadly acceptable working definition of leadership could be that:

Leadership is a process whereby an individual influences a group of individuals to attain a common goal.

One might ask quite reasonably how this is different from management? The role of the manager can be thought of as effectively to control all the existing organisational resources with a view to best delivering the existing mission (see Chapter 2 for an extensive discussion of the whole field). The role of the leader can be seen as to envision the future and any necessary new initiatives with a view to delivering the mission in changed circumstances. We might say that this role is transformational and the former is transactional. Of course, individuals are capable of undertaking both roles and typically do so to a greater or lesser extent. But the more senior the individual or the more dynamic the local circumstances the more needful it is that leadership is the primary role.

TRADITIONAL APPROACHES TO LEADERSHIP

An intuitively appealing approach to how leadership happens and the one which is most often adopted by people generally, is the so-called

Trait approach. This focuses exclusively on the leader, not at all on the followers nor the situation. It identifies traits which if possessed by a person will intrinsically enable them to be effective leaders. Traits often listed are such as intelligence, self-confidence, determination, and integrity. Thus, finding those traits in an employee would identify their potential to be a leader. On the other hand, there is no definitive and objectively established, list of such traits. Therefore, we may ask whether possession of a suitable trait really guarantees willingness to be a leader or an aptitude for leadership. Secondly, can the trait approach be correct given that no account is taken of the followers, who after all are the ones who do the work? Also, we may ask if it can possibly be true that any traits possessed would fit the person having the traits to lead in all possible situations?

It is perhaps more sophisticated to suggest that leaders must have a set of suitable skills, as well as these enabling traits, so that effective leadership depends on a set of technical, human, and conceptual skills. Then, at junior levels technical and human skills would be most important whereas at higher management levels human and conceptual skills would be most important. This is known as the **Leadership Skills** approach to understanding leadership. A positive aspect of this is that skills can be learnt, developed, and improved, thus providing a route map to becoming a leader, giving us a structure for leadership education. But of course, it is only a development of the fundamental trait approach.

A MORE CONTEMPORARY AND REALISTIC VIEW OF LEADERSHIP

McChrystal[2] develops what seems to be a much more realistic view of the Leadership process (Figure 8.1).

The proposal is that leadership is in fact a dynamic system in which leaders, followers and the situation (culturally mediated and made up of both task and context) interact continuously. What we call leadership is then a system property which emerges from this interplay and will vary constantly as the elements of the system vary. Leadership is not so much what the leader provides personally rather it is the system of organisational direction, leading ultimately to the success or failure of the organisational mission. This is a **Contingent Theory** of leadership, as are those in the following sections, in which it follows that we should consider how leaders may react so as to be successful in different situations that lead to differences in the task and how leaders should manage the relationship between themselves and their followers, who of course, react also to situational variables.

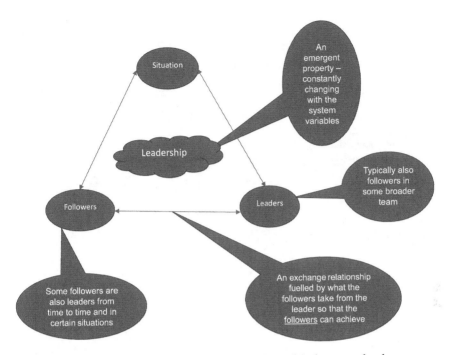

Figure 8.1 Leadership as a property of the relationship between leaders, followers and situation adapted from McChrystal, S., Eggars, J. and Mangone, J. *Leaders: Myths and Reality*, Penguin (2019).

THE LEADER FOLLOWER RELATIONSHIP

The **Relational Perspective** on leadership, known also as the **Leader-Member Exchange (LMX)**[3] approach focuses on the vertical one-to-one linkage between the leader and follower. It moves the focus away from being solely on the leader or situation, both of which approaches tend to treat followers as an undifferentiated group. LMX looks at the separate relationship between the leader and each follower, taking the view that leadership is a process centred on interactions between leaders and individual followers who are of course not all the same. Clearly the leader should be seeking to build high-quality relationships with as many followers as possible for highest overall performance. How might this be done? Graen and Uhi-Bien (1991) propose that it occurs over a three-phase process starting from the leader and follower being strangers and leading to having developed a partnership towards achieving their joint objectives (Figure 8.2).

Equally, it will be clear from what was said above that the leader cannot focus solely on these relationships, and nor does the leader want the

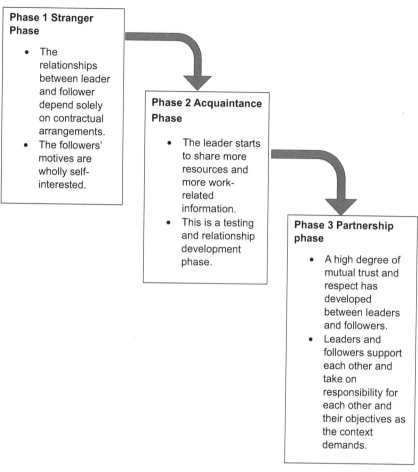

Figure 8.2 A proposed three-phase process in which the leader and follower move from being strangers to being partners focused on their shared objectives adapted from Graen and Uhi-Bien (1991).

follower to do this either. At all times account must also be taken of the situation and the task (see Figure 8.1).

SITUATION-RELATED LEADERSHIP STYLES

The idea here is that leaders should focus on understanding and adapting to varying situations subject to their followers' abilities to deal with them. That is, the leader changes their style of leadership depending on the competences and commitment level of the followers in the context of the situation. Thus, Hersey and Blanchard[4] recommend that a leader's style should be flexible adapting to the developmental and commitment level of their followers. The style of leadership adopted should then optimise subordinate performance and maximises task achievement. To do this, they propose that leaders adopt one of four basic styles, **Directive, Coaching, Supportive or Delegating** according to the competence and commitment of the followers in the current situation. Figure 8.3 sets out the relationship between these variables.

One might ask however whether all leaders can adopt all these very different styles, it is perhaps more likely that this is not the case. Accordingly, this approach is best used to offer a rule of thumb for use by more senior managers seeking to identify which leaders are best for which situations. Assessment of the team competence/commitment situation is however, clearly subjective and care in this would be needed as an incorrectly assessed situation would result in incorrect judgements about what kind of leader was required and consequent organisational failures. To give a perhaps extreme example, a team which was highly competent and committed and hence used to a great degree of delegated responsibility would not be likely to respond well to a new leader who had a very directing approach. Of course, it might be that there

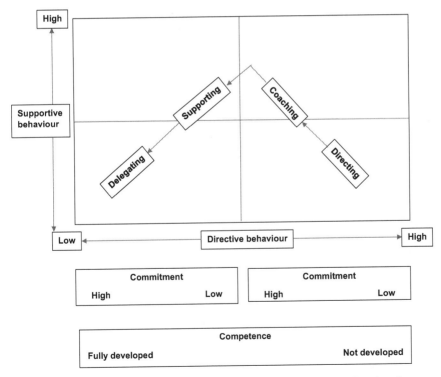

Figure 8.3 Leadership styles model adapted from Hersey and Blanchard.

was an urgent need to change the team's activities but as is made clear in the following chapter the change management outcomes would be unpredictable at best.

TASK-RELATED LEADERSHIP BEHAVIOURS

So far, we have discussed theoretical approaches to what leadership consists of and what leaders do. In the end however the purpose of a leader is to provide direction to the work of an organisation such that its objectives are achieved. It would appear important therefore to consider the practical steps that leaders might take, what behaviours they might realistically adopt, which are likely to result in positive outcomes in the context of highly complex and often dynamic organisational environments, both internally and externally to the organisation.

GENERAL PRINCIPLES FOR LEADERSHIP

These principles are adapted from the UK Army Principles of War[5] and seek to address the points made in the preceding paragraph.

The principles are said to be enduring, but not immutable nor absolute nor prescriptive. The relative importance of each may vary according to context and their application requires judgement, common sense, and intelligent interpretation. However, the first principle has always been thought to be pre-eminent and the second principle is usually considered more important than the remainder. These latter are not otherwise listed in any order of importance. Of course, leaders also need to consider the legitimacy of all actions taken by them and their followers, based on the legal, moral, and ethical propriety of the proposed action.

1. **Selection and Maintenance of the Aim** – A single, unambiguous aim is the keystone of all successful operations. Determination to maintain this aim despite difficulties until it is achieved is fundamental to success – but this is also a recipe for groupthink and consequent catastrophes, if the following principles are not also always fully considered.
2. **Maintenance of Morale** – Morale is a positive state of mind derived from inspiring leadership, a shared sense of purpose and values, well-being, perceptions of worth and group cohesion. In other words, creation of a motivated group and a positive organisational culture. No aims of whatever sort can be achieved by a demoralised organisation.

3. **Offensive Action** – Offensive action is the way in which a leader seeks to gain competitive advantage to sustain momentum and to seize the initiative. To operate wholly defensively is to guarantee ultimate failure, at best a process of managed decline. The external environment of all organisations is constantly changing, new risks, new opportunities and new competitors arise continuously, requiring the organisation itself continuously to change.

4. **Security** – Security is the provision and maintenance of an operating environment that affords the necessary freedom of action to achieve objectives while not taking undue risks. An appropriate balance of risk and reward must be established and always maintained. The balance between risk and reward continuously varies, consequent upon the changing external environment.

5. **Surprise** – Surprise generates competitive advantage as the consequence of shock and confusion induced by the new and the unexpected. Innovation and creativity in approach, process, policy, and product or service are all means to this end.

6. **Concentration of Force** – Concentration of force involves the decisive, synchronised application of resources and competences to realise intended outcomes. Dispersion of effort across a wide range of activities that are unfocused on the main aim is wasteful of time, energy, and resources, all of which are always limited. Such dispersion leads to competitive advantage being frittered away.

7. **Economy of Effort** – Economy of effort is the judicious exploitation of resources and time in relation to the achievement of objectives. Wasteful deployment of these resources will unbalance the risk/reward ratio and require the commitment of reserves earlier than otherwise. Note that once reserves have been committed they must be rebuilt as a matter of urgency to ensure the continued resilience of the organisation to the unexpected threat or opportunity.

8. **Flexibility** – Flexibility is the ability of the organisation to change readily to meet new circumstances and comprises agility, responsiveness, resilience, acuity, and adaptability. An inflexible organisation will not be able, in a timely way, to respond to competitor's actions or changes in the environment.

9. **Cooperation** – Cooperation entails teamwork and a sharing of burdens, risks, and opportunities.

10. **Sustainability** – To sustain an organisation is to generate the means by which its competitive advantage and freedom of action are maintained.

MISSION LEADERSHIP

Mission Leadership[6] is not a new idea either; it reflects the command structure of most successful military forces throughout modern history. The idea is to allow large and complex organisations to act with speed and cohesion despite a complex and chaotic environment. Nonmilitary organisations do not face these difficulties to the same extent but nevertheless there is a valuable lesson to be learnt.

For all organisations there are gaps between what a plan intends and what actually happens, gaps between the expected outcomes from our actions and the actual outcomes, and between what we expect people to do and what they actually do. The more complex the organisation and the more dynamic and competitive the environment the bigger these gaps will be. The challenge is to succeed despite these gaps. Detailed control from a senior level cannot ever address these problems, most likely it just makes them worse. On the other hand, trusted, confident and motivated leaders close to the location of actions and outcomes can improve organisational performance.

A key set of leadership practices and behaviours can enable this happy outcome in which the gaps referred to previously can be reduced significantly, albeit not eliminated.

- **Senior leaders give broad direction**, simply and clearly, rather than issuing detailed orders while junior leaders are encouraged to use their initiative to exploit opportunity that arise and to aid and support each other.
- **Orders are replaced by missions** which explain what is to be achieved and why – setting out a task and a purpose.
- **Senior leaders do not interfere** with junior leaders' activities. They trust the junior leader to work effectively towards the mission.
- The **junior leader decides how to deliver the mission** in the circumstances they themselves face. They must be willing to use the freedom they have been granted and prepared to accept responsibility and not try to reverse delegate it back upwards.
- **All levels report back very regularly** on actions and progress, creating a cycle of positive feedback and continuous adjustment.

In this way, the clear and simple description of the mission enables actions of a large and complex organisation to be coherent. Giving the junior leaders a wide measure of freedom within the constraints of task and purpose enables a flexible response to developing circumstances as, when and where that development occurs.

Organisational benefits accruing from this approach include:

- Increased clarity and alignment as strategy is understood by all, and all translate this into their own actions.
- Increased speed and effectiveness as resources are focused where they are really needed, management hesitation decreases, and decision making time shortens.
- Initiatives are taken as necessary as people adapt their own actions to changes in their situation.
- Consequently, the organisation can change course at speed.
- Leaders and teams throughout the organisation are motivated by a strong feeling of self-actualising achievement. Leader motivation comes through the opportunity of all leaders at every level to make a distinct contribution to the collective purpose.

TOXIC LEADERSHIP

Any leader may face difficulties that turn out to be beyond the resources of the organisation to deal with, but some leaders seem to promote activities that are themselves seen to carry the seeds of failure. Sometimes, this can be so serious that the negative outcomes are very destructive for the organisation and for individual stakeholders. This has been referred to as **Toxic Leadership**.[7] These negative and particularly destructive consequences emerge from a confluence of the style and personality of the leader, from susceptible followers, and from conducive environments.

Observable destructive leadership behaviours may indicate that this situation exists in advance of destructive organisational outcomes becoming generally apparent. Behaviours that may be seen are such as:

- Micromanagement – the leader defines and then supervises the task in every detail.
- Control above all – the fundamental leadership style is to seek to ensure complete personal control of all activity.
- Threatening behaviours – these may be physical such as dominating a person's space or verbal often including insult used as a management tool or humour used to demean and denigrate.

For toxic leaders to take control, they need an environment where they can thrive. Elements that contribute towards a conducive environment include:

- Instability within the organisation.
- Perceived external threat to the organisation.
- Questionable values and standards forming the organisational culture.

Equally followers would need to be susceptible to the approach taken by the toxic leader. This may arise in two main ways.

- *Conformers* are passive in the face of toxic leadership. Typically, they lack confidence and feel the need for an authority figure to provide them with security.
- *Colluders* are proactive and wilfully accept toxic leadership. They are personally ambitious and prepared to act in whatever way will be necessary and so will imitate toxic behaviours to become toxic leaders themselves.

It is notable here that the existence of such susceptible followers in a team is most unlikely to be conducive to good team performance in general. Conformers will not be innovative and creative and will tend to accelerate the appearance of groupthink. Colluders certainly are not team players and will try to direct the team to move in ways which promote their own personal ambitions.

ETHICAL LEADERSHIP – AN ANTIDOTE TO TOXICITY

Leadership is a process of influencing so that the leader will impact the lives of others. This carries with it an ethical burden and responsibility. Leaders are more powerful than the led so leaders have a great responsibility to be sensitive to how their leadership affects followers' lives. Thus, leadership is not and cannot ever be amoral and without values.

This thinking builds on principles discussed and developed over thousands of years across all the philosophical traditions of the world. Furthermore, there is copious practical evidence from history, from ancient to very recent, of the disastrous consequences for the organisation and all its stakeholders of ignoring these points, seeking to take shortcuts, indulging in cover-ups, or holding that the ends justify the means. Such approaches can never end well.

Northouse[8] offers a model of what constitutes ethical leadership and which can be set down in the following advice for leaders:

- **Respect others.**
  - Treat others as ends in themselves, never as means.
  - Listen closely to other points of view treating all as worthy.
- **Serve others.**
  - Contribute to the greater good in ways that benefit all not self.
  - Be follower centred placing interests of others foremost.

- **Be just.**
  - Fairness is at the centre of decision making.
  - Differences in treatment must be clearly and reasonably justified and based on moral values.

- **Be honest.**
  - Dishonesty destroys trust and is always found out.
  - Maintain a predisposition to open and candid behaviour while balancing this with what is appropriate to disclose in any situation.

- **Build community.**
  - Focusing on the common good, the shared goal.
  - Taking account of the purposes of everyone involved.
  - Demonstrating civic virtue, social responsibility.

A SUMMARY OF EVIDENCE FROM THE EXPERIENCES OF GREAT LEADERS OF THE PAST

There exist many memoirs and histories of the activities of successful leaders of the past, generally in the political and military fields of endeavour. We have seen above that leadership is about influencing people to act to achieve some outcome and, of course, people's behaviour has not changed at all in the relatively few years in which history has been written. There have been massive technological advances, but human nature remains exactly as it always was. It is sometimes argued[9] that human nurture has developed considerably over the last thousand years or so, especially those years since around 1000 CE, resulting in greater self-awareness and willingness to show initiative and take risks for personal advancement (as seen in Maslow's idea of self-actualisation as the peak human need). But this would apply to the leader just as much as the follower.

There is potentially much of value to be gained from studying the experiences and ideas of past leaders. To do so thoroughly is the work of a lifetime but given below, as a starting point, is a selection from some very well-known historical figures.

SITUATION-RELATED ADVICE

In order to govern, the question is not to follow out a more or less valid theory but to build with whatever materials are at hand. The inevitable must be accepted and turned to advantage.

Napoleon Bonaparte

Time is a sort of river of passing events, and strong is its current; no sooner is a thing brought to sight than it is swept by and another takes its place, and this too will be swept away.

Marcus Aurelius

FOLLOWER-RELATED ADVICE

A leader is a dealer in hope.

There are only two forces in the world, the sword and the spirit. In the long run the sword will always be conquered by the spirit.

Napoleon Bonaparte

Box 8.2 Adapted from Wikipedia accessed on 31/10/2023

Napoleon Bonaparte (15 August 1769–5 May 1821) was a French military commander and political leader who rose to prominence during the French Revolution and led successful campaigns during the Revolutionary Wars. He was the leader of the French Republic from 1799 to 1804, then of the French Empire from 1804 until 1814, and briefly again in 1815. Napoleon's political and cultural legacy endures as a celebrated and controversial leader. He initiated many liberal reforms that have persisted and is considered one of the greatest military commanders in history. His campaigns are still studied at military academies worldwide.

Wars may be fought with weapons, but they are won by men. It is the spirit of men who follow and of the man who leads that gains the victory.

George S. Patton

Box 8.3 Adapted from Wikipedia Accessed on 31/10/2023

George Smith Patton Jr.(11 November 1885–21 December 1945) was a general in the United States Army who commanded the Seventh United States Army in the Mediterranean and the Third United States Army in France and Germany after the invasion of Normandy in June 1944 His emphasis on rapid and aggressive offensive action proved effective, and he was regarded highly by his opponents in the German High Command.

The true test of a leader is whether his followers will adhere to his cause from their own volition, enduring the most arduous hardships without being forced to do so, and remaining steadfast in the moments of greatest peril.

Xenophon

Box 8.4 Adapted from Wikipedia Accessed on 31/10/2023

Xenophon (c. 430 – probably 355 or 354 BC]) was a Greek military leader, philosopher, and historian, born in Athens. At the age of 30, Xenophon was elected commander of one of the biggest Greek mercenary armies of the Achaemenid Empire, the Ten Thousand, that marched on and came close to capturing Babylon in 401 BC. Xenophon established precedents for many logistical operations, and was among the first to describe strategic flanking manoeuvres and feints in combat.

LEADER-RELATED ADVICE

Everything we hear is an opinion, not a fact. Everything we see is a perspective, not the truth.

Marcus Aurelius

Box 8.5 Adapted from Wikipedia Accessed on 31/10/2023

Marcus Aurelius (26 April 121–17 March 180) was Roman emperor from 161 to 180 AD and a Stoic philosopher. He was the last of the rulers later known as the Five Good Emperors, and the last emperor of the Pax Romana, an age of relative peace, calm, and stability for the Roman Empire.

The truest wisdom is a resolute determination.
He who fears being conquered is sure of defeat.
Take time to deliberate, but when the time for action has arrived, stop thinking and go in

Napoleon Bonaparte

Sure I am of this, that you have only to endure to conquer.

Winston Churchill

Box 8.6 Adapted from Wikipedia Accessed on 31/10/2023

Sir Winston Leonard Spencer Churchill (30 November 1874–24 January 1965) was a British statesman, soldier, and writer who served as Prime Minister of the United Kingdom twice, from 1940 to 1945 during the Second World War, and again from 1951 to 1955. Widely considered one of the 20th century's most significant figures, Churchill remains popular in the United Kingdom, where he is generally viewed as a victorious wartime leader who played an important role in defending liberal democracy against the spread of fascism. While he has been criticised for his views on race and empire alongside some of his wartime decisions, historians often rank Churchill as the greatest prime minister in British history.

Don't tell people how to do things, tell them what needs to be done and let them surprise you with their results.
We herd sheep, we drive cattle, we lead people.

George S. Patton

Never give an order that can't be obeyed.
The best luck of all is the luck you make for yourself.

Douglas MacArthur

Box 8.7 Adapted from Wikipedia Accessed on 31/10/2023

Douglas MacArthur (26 January 1880–5 April 1964) was an American military leader who served as General of the Army for the United States. He served with distinction in World War I, was Chief of Staff of the United States Army during the 1930s and played a prominent role in the Pacific during World War II. He was one of only five men to rise to the rank of General of the Army in the U.S. Army.

REBECCA RAWNSLEY – A MODERN MANAGEMENT CAREER

Q Thinking of all the leaders you've worked for in your career, what have been their key characteristics that valued?

A key characteristic of a leader, for me, would be being supportive but also being willing to say clearly what needs to be said. So, to share information, not hide it, even if it's not the best news to deliver. I have had leaders who gave me a lot of backing and support, so I knew that I was trusted, within the boundaries, to get on with doing something. Honest feedback on performance is then important saying, you know, next time, I think you should look at how you do this or that. Helping me to develop.

Q Summarising then; clarity, honesty, and support. Would that be your top three?

Yes, I think they would.

Q What about the other side of the coin. What are the things which make it very difficult to be led by someone?

I think if they are insecure as a leader. That makes it incredibly difficult. So, I guess confidence should go in with the clarity, honesty, and support. Insecurity shows in their management style, typically they want to know and be involved in everything. They have a micro-management approach. They tend to keep information to themselves and hold on to contacts with other leaders or departments. Then, because of that, they also do not give back-up to their team because they are also protecting themselves. From a business point of view, that just slows everything down. Certainly, I have struggled with that type of leader because then I am questioning their role, if they are spending all their time checking what's going on, what are they doing, what are they contributing? At most, that is acting as a post box. One thing I have noticed is that sort of leader tends not even to refer to you by name, I would be referred to just as "my bid manager". You are hidden in the team, like you were just a resource.

Q OK, so those are key characteristics, positive and negative. Now, when you moved from being a member of a team to being a leader of the team, what did you think you had to develop yourself into the role?

Well, one thing I had to develop was an ability at delegation. Also, you cannot have perfectionist expectations of your team. Good is good enough so long as the next time is better. I was letting go of the day-to-day and giving the others the opportunities that I was given. Taking a step back so others could step up.

Q So this is what the insecure leaders you mentioned earlier did not do, they had retained their grasp of the day-to-day?

Yes, they had not made that transition. It is not easy. Your new role is about trying to get initiatives, improvements, underway and garnering support. Support for your team and improvements for the business. You must have trust in your people and let them get on and just say I'm here if you need me. Run the show, it is yours.

Q One of the things discussed in leadership studies is the different styles of leadership that exist and how what is needed depends on the circumstances as well as on the characteristics of the leader themselves. What is your view on the idea that leaders can adopt different styles according to the situation?

I am not so sure about it, your personality will and should, come through. You can manage the team a little differently, say in moments of urgency. But I think your leadership style is driven from you and your personality and your learning from experience over the years.

Q OK, you would say that it is to do with your traits, your inbuilt traits as a person plus your experience. But does that mean that there are people who cannot ever be leaders.

I think that most people can identify bits of their own personality which could be used successfully to manage, that is to be successful transactionally. But leading is about transformation and vision. Even if nothing radical is on the immediate horizon the leader must ask how to motivate the team, how make them feel valued, special? You must be there for your people and looking to improve performance. Of course, people do not have to become either a leader or a manager to progress. In a well-run organisation you can still progress as an individual in your field of expertise.

Q Yes, but do those people ever get frustrated because they cannot be in a decision-making role?

I think there can be some frustration, and some might wonder, if the progression they have achieved is just a token? But still it must be done in the in the best way possible for retention and motivation.

Q Right, now I want to try and put you on the spot and ask what is the single most important thing that a person should be good at if they're going to be a good leader; what would you say?

Emotional intelligence linked to communication skills would be my answer. Also to have a vision which you can bring people along towards. A lot of people would say charisma but that can be negative too. Hitler was charismatic it seems. I think it is the ability to communicate because you need to communicate with your people you need to communicate upwards, you need to make sure that everyone is aware of what is going on. But of course, you must deliver the message in very different ways for different people.

Q So, as a leader you are the channel of communications and there need to be good interpersonal skills and emotional intelligence.

Yes, you need to sometimes break not the nicest of news without creating complete demotivation. It is not just the communication skills of the PR; it is the ability to read the room. To deliver the message in the right way, to find the right channels of communication. All the while with the objective of elevating the performance of the team.

THE CHAPTER EXAMPLE CASE – MEL

Sarah faced the challenge of leading a team of change managers – something she had never done before. She wondered what the best way might be to think about this new role? Sarah felt that in her own field of CRM she had a well-developed Mission Leadership approach to her team all of whom were well trained and committed to the team goals. But the change management team was new and the members, while selected for their apparent commitment and skills were rather an unknown quantity. Weighing this up it appeared to Sarah that she would do well to consider the advice of Hersey and Blanchard[10] around selecting an appropriate style of leadership to fit the circumstances. They recommend that.

- A leader's style should be flexible.
- Leaders should adapt their style according to the developmental and commitment level of their followers.
- Leaders should adopt a style of leadership that optimises subordinate performance and maximises task achievement.

The change agents had been selected for their commitment and their knowledge and skills relevant to the work of their own parts of MEL but so far as Sarah knew none of them had previous experience of managing major organisational change. It had to be assumed therefore that their level of development from her point of view as leader of a change team was currently low. It seemed likely that the change proposed would meet significant challenges along the way. Some of these challenges would be localised around a particular change agent, and others would be more general albeit showing a particular face in each department. Hersey and Blanchard suggest Sarah would need to lead the change process by giving clear direction and lots of support to the change agents, coaching them to develop their change management skills. Over time, the direction she would need to give would become less, allowing her eventually to delegate to each change agent a full change leadership role in their own area so that then she would be able to focus on the overall organisational success of implementing the new strategy.

CHAPTER CASE: SERGIO MARCHIONNE – SAVIOUR OF FIAT

In 2008, Sergio Marchionne said that Fiat had been a laughingstock when he was appointed CEO, four years earlier. Speaking to the *Harvard Business Review* he said

> Whenever you opened a newspaper in Italy, there was another embarrassing story: Fiat had lost more money; its new car had flopped; a strike was on somewhere. Even more worrying to me was the fact that the company had gone through four CEOs in three years. Imagine showing up in June 2004 and being the fifth guy to try to resuscitate what appeared to most people to be a cadaver.

Sergio Marchionne came from outside the car industry to be the new leader. He knew that the automotive industry was an incredibly tough business. Most car companies, with a few exceptions such as Toyota in Japan and Porsche in Germany, have consistently destroyed value over the years. Fiat was one of the worst offenders.

Four years later the bottom line was solidly in the black and there had been some major changes made to the way the company ran. Marchionne had sought to abandon the Great Man model of leadership that long characterised Fiat and created a culture where everyone was expected to lead. He said of his job,

> .... it is not to make decisions about the business but to set stretch objectives and help our managers work out how to reach them.

Fiat had had a leadership problem. Traditionally, all important decisions in Italian companies were made by the CEO. The existing senior leadership below the CEO was not used to taking responsibility. A business such as Fiat is far too large and complicated for one man alone to lead. Marchionne discovered that the company had lots of hidden talent at more junior levels, around the world away from the Italian HQ and in fields other than the traditionally accepted training grounds of engineering roles.

At first, he found these people himself by visiting plants, walking about and talking to people. Later, he set up processes, under control of HR to identify people with high potential.

He then spent a lot of time engaging informally with them. Doing this, he was mainly interested in how well they lead people and lead change. Marchionne said about these people:

.... know that I care about what happens to them. If the organization can feel that kind of connection with its leadership, you're going to get a pretty sound culture aligned around strongly held common values...... alongside more responsibility must come more accountability. However, it is important to recognise that objectives will be missed, markets and economies aren't perfectly predictable, but, if you want to grow leaders, you can't let explanations and excuses become a way of life.

After his death in 2018 The Financial Times wrote

Sergio Marchionne .... deserved to be called a leader. He had a vision of what needed to be done to return a troubled company and industry to health, worked relentlessly to realise it, and brought many others along with him. .... He will be remembered more for the way he did the job: sticking to his own strategic vision in the face of risk and criticism, speaking his mind plainly, demanding the most from himself and his team, and always holding himself accountable. This model of leadership saved two companies from failure. The reason more leaders do not follow it is probably because so few have the energy, intelligence and will of Marchionne.

Sources: Harvard Business Review, December 2008,
Financial Times, July 2018.

CASE DISCUSSION QUESTIONS

1. What kind of leader was Sergio Marchionne?
2. Analyse the evidence of Sergio Marchionne's leadership activities using the models presented in the chapter.

CLASS DISCUSSION QUESTIONS

1. The traits approach to leadership is widely criticised, but at the same time, it seems to have a strong link to human intuition. What are your views on this?
2. Leadership skills might be said to be nothing more than traits of the leader. Do you agree?
3. The transformational model of leadership emphasises the importance of followers. Why?
4. Outline and critically evaluate the work on Leadership done by Hersey and Blanchard giving examples.
5. Mission Leadership is directly relevant to the real world of organisational direction. Critically evaluate this statement.
6. What factors enable the toxicity of leadership. Are they inevitable to some degree?
7. Explain the meaning of the term "ethical leadership". Is it a realistic concept in the real world of organisational management?

CHAPTER SUMMARY

- Leadership is a process whereby an individual influences a group of individuals to attain a common goal.
- Leadership is the process of organisational direction, leading ultimately to the success or failure of the organisational mission. Leaders must react appropriately to be successful in different situations and to manage the relationship between themselves and their followers.
- Leaders may adopt one of four basic styles, **Directive, Coaching, Supportive or Delegating** according to the competence and commitment of their followers given the current situation.

- Leadership is unlikely to be successful unless there is a single, unambiguous aim. Determination to maintain this aim despite difficulties is fundamental to success.
- Leadership is unlikely to be successful unless morale is maintained. No aims of whatever sort are likely to be achieved by a demoralised organisation.
- The Mission Leadership approach allows large and complex organisations to act with speed and cohesion despite a complex and chaotic environment.
- Leaders are more powerful than the led, so leaders have a great responsibility to be sensitive to how their leadership affects followers' lives. Leadership is not and cannot be amoral and without values it must be always ethical.

NOTES

1 Northouse, P.G. (2019) *Leadership Theory and Practice*, London: Sage.
2 Mcchrystal, S., Eggars, J. and Mangone, J. (2019) *Leaders: Myths and Reality*, London: Penguin.
3 Northouse, P.G. (2019) *Leadership Theory and Practice*, London: Sage.
4 Hersey, P. and Blanchard, K.H. (1969) Life cycle theory of leadership. *Training & Development Journal*, 23(5): 26–34.
5 British Defence Doctrine, Joint Doctrine Publication 0-01 (JDP 0-01) (4th Ed.) dated November 2011.
6 Bungay, S. (2011) *Art of Action: How Leaders Close the Gaps between Plans, Actions and Results*, New Town Square, PA: Project Management Institute.
7 Whicker, M.L. (1996) *Toxic Leaders: When Organizations Go Bad*, Westport, CT : Quorum Books.
8 Northouse, P.G. (2019) *Leadership Theory and Practice*, London: Sage.
9 Mortimer, I. (2024) *Medieval Horizons*, London: Penguin Random House.
10 Hersey, P. and Blanchard, K.H. (1969) Life cycle theory of leadership. *Training & Development Journal*, 23(5): 26–34.

9 The Manager as Leader of Change

INTRODUCTION

All organisations are subject to continuous change. It may be of internal or external origin, it may be big or small, it may be fast or slow, it may be like past experiences, or it may be unprecedented. Whichever of these describes the current change it cannot be ignored, and it is the job of managers to reset organisational operations appropriately. Indeed, to manage is, most importantly, to manage change. To fail to manage change is to doom the organisation to ultimate failure. Referring back to the previous chapter, this is where the manager must most necessarily be in a leadership role.

ORIGINS OF CHANGE

Firstly, change may arise outside the organisation. Strategists and marketers refer to a PESTEL[1] model of the external environment. This stands for six key forces that drive major types of change in the World: Political Change, Economic Change, Social Change, Technological Change, Ecological Change and Legal Change. These changes are often very powerful and operating in the long term and are certainly beyond the strength of an individual organisation to mitigate other than very marginally. Instead, organisations must identify the Opportunities and Threats which arise from them and design internal changes to avoid the latter and take advantage of the former. Organisations operating in any sort of competitive environment must also consider the competitive Opportunities and Threats arising in their markets (usually they apply a model called Porter's Five Forces) and must act in the same way in relation to these.

DOI: 10.4324/9781032686592-9

Of course, there will also be continuous processes of internal change. These relate to all parts of the organisational operation:

- People are recruited, learn, and develop and eventually leave the organisation taking their experience, relationships, contacts, intellect, and energy with them.
- Research and Development and the changing needs of customers, suppliers and partners lead to new products and services created in new ways.
- Financial circumstances change as debt becomes due or sales increase or decrease in value etc.

To a significant degree a manager can have some control over these changes although many may happen under the radar so to speak. There is also the danger that managers, because of this ability to exert some control, will over focus on these internal changes at the expense of the external, a case of not being able to see the wood for the trees. The self-confidence and pride that a manager will feel in a job well done may also lead to a wilful inability to see what is changing and what the consequences may be.

Then there are stakeholders, both internal and external, who are sometimes more and sometimes less interested and sometimes weaker or more powerful in relation to organisations. Managers must keep a close eye on changes in the relative position and interests of all stakeholders noting that the changes occurring in the environment or internally will impact the stakeholders too and this will cause a second-order impact on the organisation.

ADDRESSING THE NEED TO IMPLEMENT OUR RESPONSE TO CHANGE

Deciding on how to deal with all this change is all very well and very challenging but it is of no value if decisions on how to respond are not then successfully implemented through a process of managed organisational change. This is difficult. The organisational change itself may be complex and thereby complicated to implement but, additionally, the context, internally and externally is uncertain and subject to further continuous change.

Changes we are making in our organisation may be big or small but to some extent they will impact the relationships we have with colleagues, partners, suppliers, customers, and other key stakeholders. It is possibly intended to create changes in these relationships but probably not in all such relationships, presenting the additional problem that we may well need to protect some aspects of our organisation from the changes we ourselves are making.

Most importantly of all and creating most difficulty and potential failure modes, is the fact that organisational change will always require the people who work in the organisation to modify what they do, how they do it, when they do it and with whom they do it. On the whole, people do not want to change their everyday life unless they can see a very good reason to do so and hence it is likely that changes will be resisted, at least passively and likely actively. So, we need to do a complex thing in an uncertain situation and subject to resisting forces. How shall we do this? The answer is by leading a carefully planned and implemented organisational change management process to a successful outcome.

CHANGE MANAGEMENT – AN OUTLINE

Change Management is a subject on which there is a very extensive theoretical literature, what follows here is a brief outline of some key points.

Box 9.1

Schein (1990) described change as

> the induction of new patterns of action, belief and attitudes among substantial segments of the population.

He stated a set of assumptions about the organisational inertia which would need to be overcome to make this happen:

- Change involves people in learning new things and unlearning old things, these latter are possibly important parts of their personality and social relationships.
- Change requires that there is a motivation to change.
- Organisational change is always mediated through individual change.
- Change often evokes strong emotions of fear and uncertainty.
- Change consists of many stages all of which must be completed before the change is completed.

Change is concerned with people and their tasks, just like everything else in this book. In the end therefore, the delivery of change will be about leadership. Notice that we are not here dealing with trivial change such as purchase of a new machine or a new factory, but the much more difficult challenge of getting people to move to the new factory! We shall see that the role of the leader in this includes a number of key elements such as

- Searching for opportunities and exploring different approaches
- Initiating Change & Innovation
  - Conceptualising the change process
  - Crystallising the future in plans and as a vision
- Enabling Change & Innovation
  - Organising and initiating the practical work to make change happen.
  - Valuing people's contributions, supporting people to change and acknowledging people's fears and anxieties.
  - Establishing a positive climate for change and ultimate adoption of a new set of activities.

This set of leadership activities is often called **Transformational.** That is leadership with a view to inspiring followers to achieve new things in new ways. Transformational leaders are **change agents.** They are good role models who can create and articulate a clear vision and empower, enthuse, and motivate followers. They give their followers a feeling of hope, an anticipation of a better future.

FIRST STEPS

The first step then is to consider what scale of change is being attempted and what therefore may be an appropriate style of change management. Scale in this sense refers firstly to the impact of the change on the organisation, is it a relatively minor realignment or is it wholly transformational and secondly to the intended speed of the change from very gradual to immediate. Minor organisational change happens all the time and is inevitable being driven by relatively minor internal and external forces. If this is gradual it is likely to meet less resistance but if it is sudden, it can be difficult to handle even if it is of little real consequence. On the other hand, strategic change occurs more rarely but is large scale, complex and difficult in itself and likely to meet with substantial resistance.

Considering these two scales of size and speed we might set out four possible types of change (adapted from Balogun and Hailey[2]):

- Adaptation – a very gradual adjustment of the existing parts of the organisation to be able to do new things with existing resources and competences.

- Evolution – a very gradual development of all or most aspects of the organisation towards some totally different activities using new resources and competences.
- Reconstruction – an immediate reconstruction of the existing parts of the organisation to be able to do new things with existing resources and competences.
- Revolution – an immediate transformation of all or most aspects of the organisation towards some totally different activities using new resources and competences.

There are also several lesser albeit often important factors to consider:

- Preservation – the need to protect parts of the organisation from inadvertent changes caused by the changes undertaken elsewhere.
- Diversity – the need to consider how changes we make will have a different impact on parts of our organisation where other organisational cultures prevail.
- Capacity to change – existence of the resources required to make the change real.
- Readiness to change – at all levels and in all parts of the organisation.

In general, people will be less comfortable if change is rapid and if change is large so that Revolutionary change will create the most psychological discomfort and Adaptive change the least. When the level of discomfort is high it can be anticipated that the resistance to change will be high. It can be seen that there are four main reasons for that resistance, all of which must be considered by those seeking to lead a change:

- Self-interest – people who believe that the change will cause them to lose something they value.
- Misunderstandings – people misunderstanding the impact of the proposed change; this is most likely to occur when there is a lack of trust within the organisation.
- Different assessments of the need for change or the impact of the change – diverse constituencies will probably assess things differently from each other.
- Low tolerance for change – all people are limited in their ability to change but the variance in this is large; a particular problem is that many people may lack confidence in their own ability to acquire necessary new skills and behaviours.

STYLES OF MANAGING CHANGE

In the light of all this we can then seek to choose one of several different styles of managing change. Firstly, as listed below by considering the urgency of the change and the degree to which the organisation as a whole and its people are ready to change.

- Education and communication – a slow process of gradual change that will minimise internal political and cultural difficulties.
- Participation and collaboration – a slow process of gradual change designed to persuade, involve and thereby, commit to change any resistant political and cultural groups within the organisation.
- Focused participation and intervention – a faster version of the above focused on the areas where change is to be most immediate and most impactful and involving direct intervention by the change management team in the design and delivery of specific local change.
- Direction – involves the issue of instructions to change enabled by the direct intervention of the change management team in the design and delivery of the changes to be made both globally and locally.
- Coercion – involves the forced replacement of any resistance by transfer or redundancy and the change management team designing and delivering the changes to be made both globally and locally.

Then, we should overlay this with consideration of the capacity to change. If this is high, then we should favour collaborative and persuasive approaches. If it is low, then we shall favour coaching ideally or direction if urgency is the key issue.

Inherent in all of this is a realisation of the fundamental importance of people-related issues in the management of change. Changing other aspects of the organisation (e.g. buying new software or leasing new premises) is trivially easy compared with changing people and their relationships, attitudes, beliefs, motivations, vision, knowledge, skills etc. This is where leadership is crucial, people follow leaders and leadership alone will determine success.

Box 9.2 Key Things for the Leader to Address in Managing Change

- Communicating the need for change – acceptance of need will help a lot to overcome resistance to change.
- Communicating the practical changes and supporting adjustment processes – helping people to understand what is changing, why it is happening and how they will be helped to change themselves to meet new requirements will be important in easing the process of change.
- Enabling effective feedback from those affected – it is crucial that the leader can understand how the changes are impacting people and how they feel about this.
- Resisting growth of the grapevine – it is crucial to know what is being thought and said, privately, about the change process and then to act to correct misunderstandings.
- Building a base of support for sustainable change – if people change superficially but do not actually accept and support the changes made then the new strategy will never operate well and is likely gradually to revert to the way things were done previously.

A TOOLKIT FOR CHANGE

Force Field Analysis

Force field analysis is a simple idea formalised in the work of Kurt Lewin[3]. He points out that there are forces driving a change and other forces opposing that same change. Change will occur when the drivers for change collectively overcome the restraining forces. If we can identify and evaluate this set of opposing forces, then we can plan how to modify them so as to enable the forces for change to exceed the restraining forces. To do this we need to find a way in which the forces can be plotted and allocated relative values thereby helping to identify the current situation and what needs to be overcome and where opportunities lie.

This is indeed a simple idea, but it is not always easy to do in real life. Usually, a diagram or tabulation is drawn as below to help visualise the whole array of forces:

Driver for change	Evaluation	Restraining force	Evaluation
Demand for better quality among key customers	+5	Shortage of suitably trained staff on labour market	−3
New process technology recently available seen as having high potential	+2	New machinery and software needed is expensive	−2
Market is growing	+3	Staff resistance to acquiring new skills	−4
		Limited internal funds	−1
Total force for change	**+10**		**−10**

Of course, most of the evaluations will be subjective but some may be more clearly established, e.g. market growth rate. Either way all should be expressed on a uniform scale, say +5 to −5 so that the overall situation can clearly be seen. In the example above the forces seem to be in balance. Can we see any ways to increase any forces for change or decrease the restraining forces?

A good starting point at this stage is roughly to assess the probability of reaching your target situation if the force field stays the same. If the chance seems to be good then the simplest way forward and simplest is usually the best in this complex field, will be to leave the forces as they are. But if that is not the case then it is necessary to draw up a practical action plan for managing the field of forces to increase the probability of reaching the target situation. In devising your action plan, remember that:

- Increasing the driving forces can often result in an increase in the resisting forces. This results in the current equilibrium not in fact changing so there is no improvement in probability of success, but the internal tension increasing, causing increased difficulties and stress possibly worsening the chances of success. Overall, then, a worse situation! Reducing the resisting forces is always preferable as this allows movement towards the desired outcomes or target situation without increasing tension.
- Group norms are an important force in shaping and resisting change – so try to work with them.

STAKEHOLDER MANAGEMENT
AND COMMITMENT PLANNING

It is perhaps an obvious thought but clearly, it will help our change process if stakeholders are more committed to help than otherwise. It is useful therefore to assess each stakeholder group to see where they stand. A tabulation such as the following is a practical methodology.

Stakeholder list	Relative power	Would actively oppose	Would not actively oppose	Would help to make the change	Would be a leader of the change
Division Heads	4			X	
Trade Unions	2	X			
Institutional shareholders	3		X		
Local community	1		X		
Customers	3			X	
Division A staff	2	X			
Division B staff Etc.	1		X		

This sort of systematic approach enables thinking about how each of the stakeholder groups might be approached to ease the process of change. For example, we might not expect to be able to get the Trades Unions to help make a change take place, but we certainly could seek ways to move their attitude to one of allowing the change. Equally, given the internal power of the Division Heads surely, we would hope to be able to find ways to persuade them to join in leading the change?

More generally the change manager should develop a view on the approach to be taken to each stakeholder group. Ideally this policy position should have been in place before the current change was initiated. Figure 9.1 illustrates the categorisation of stakeholder groups according to their relative power and their level of attention to the activities of the organisation. Each of the four categories is then identified in relation to a basic policy approach which should then be developed, for each stakeholder group, into specific activities. It is important to note that the positions of groups in this analysis are not fixed. They may change in terms of level of attention especially if something is occurring now in a field that they regard as important. Equally groups that lack power but have a high level of interest may seek partnerships with other groups to enhance their power. A group with low levels of attention but high power, typical example of this is the Government or major hands-off shareholder groups such

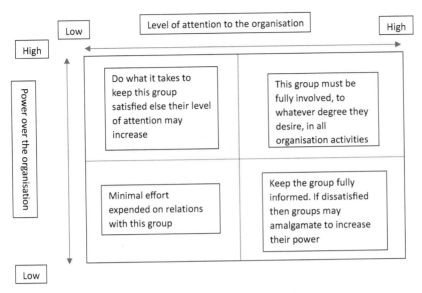

Figure 9.1 Stakeholder groups and management policy.

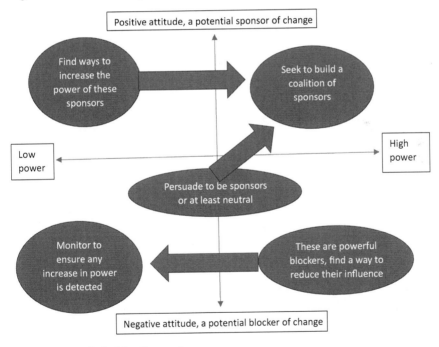

Figure 9.2 Stakeholder Strategies.

as pension funds, may become much more attentive to the organisation if it starts to do things which touch a nerve. It does not do to poke the bear.

Figure 9.2 illustrates an effective way to think about what types of activities might be useful. It takes account of the relative power of the stakeholder group in question and an assessment, necessarily subjective, of their attitude to the change proposed, positive or negative. The specific details will of course, be different in every case.

THREE PHASE MODEL FOR CHANGE

Kurt Lewin goes on to suggest a methodology for delivering change usually known as the **Three Phase Model,** as set out below. Lewin recognised that the key changes to be made and the only ones that really are difficult in the end are those around people and their attitudes.

Box 9.3 The Three Phase Model of Change

- *Phase 1*: **Unfreeze** current attitudes – recognising the need to change, even if that need is disliked, will enable a change to occur.
- *Phase 2*: **Move** to a new situation – the typical approach is to identify a series of steps which, taken together will achieve the overall change. The first of these steps should be relatively small and easy to accomplish to offer early wins that should be celebrated. In the case of each of the steps, it will be necessary to do the following:
  - Explore alternatives.
  - Identify specific obstacles to change.
  - Decide on a detailed change plan.
  - Implement plan paying special attention to people aspects.
  - Monitor progress and make corrections to details.
  - Celebrate success.
- *Phase 3*: **Refreeze** attitudes in the new situation – take steps to ensure that the changes achieved are sustainable and now represent the new working norms, thus becoming part of the Organisational Culture.

Building on the work of Lewin, Kotter[4] offers 8 "levers for change" in the form of a series of steps to be taken to deliver a change. This model has proved very successful, offering the change manager a practical set of guidelines for change planning as follows:

- Establish a sense of urgency.
- Form a powerful guiding coalition.

- Create a vision.
- Communicate the vision.
- Empower others to act on the vision.
- Create short term wins.
- Consolidate gains and build more change.
- Institutionalise the new approaches. An important part of enabling the new situation to be maintained is to demonstrate that the new situation is better for the organisation and employees, communicating success of the new arrangements with good news stories.

It is, of course, very important to monitor ongoing performance. It is always mistaken to assume that a change once made will continue to operate well or indeed, to be at all appropriate as circumstances change further, perhaps in an unexpected direction.

CHANGE AGENCY

A relatively small change in a smaller organisation may perhaps be implementable by one change manager. If the change is substantial, as strategic change typically is or if the organisation is large or perhaps unusually diverse even though small, then the change manager will need help. The change manager will need eyes and ears and voices and hands on the ground in each of the parts of the organisation, especially, but not only, in those in which the change is happening. These assistants are usually called **Change Agents**. A change agent is anyone who has the commitment, skill, and power to stimulate, facilitate, and coordinate the change effort. They may be either external or internal. The success of any change effort depends heavily on the quality and workability of the relationship between the change agent, the change manager, and the key decision makers within the organisation. An important part of planning for the change is therefore, to identify and recruit a change agent network. This can be tackled using the following steps:

- Step 1: Identify your change agents asking the questions:
  - How does change successfully happen in this organisation?
  - Which parts of this organisation need to change?
  - Who in these parts has the necessary skills and commitment?

- Step 2: Engaging your Change Agents. Your chosen change agents may or may not yet be ready to influence and make the necessary changes to develop and offer local leadership.

- Who and what will be most effective in gaining this change agent's support and interest?
- How should you approach this person to involve them in the network? What information will be most compelling to them – e.g. the market research results, your organisation's business case for the strategic change, and feedback from customers?

- Step 3: Mobilising your Change Agents to ensure that the rationale and approach for developing and embedding the change is visible throughout the organisation. Their role is to:

  - Oversee the progress of the change and help to facilitate the necessary actions each in their own area.
  - Provide a link back to the change manager and the senior decision-making team on progress being achieved.
  - Collectively take overall responsibility for the successful development and embedding of the change by delivering the necessary local changes.

A PROJECT MANAGEMENT APPROACH

Implementation planning will involve taking a **project management** approach – i.e. as was pointed out above, the planned **management of change**. Project Management is an enormous subject and is not the within the purview of this text but, in outline, we can say that it involves the following key steps.[5]

1. Define the project.
2. Build a plan.
3. Agree the plan with key stakeholders.
4. Communicate to all those involved in implementing the plan.
5. Get the work done.
6. Monitor progress and update the plan – as often as necessary.

Defining the project requires us to clarify exactly what are the objectives of our proposed change. Good clear objectives are often said to be best constructed in a **SMART** format meaning Specific, Measurable, Achievable, Relevant and Time bound. In writing our SMART objectives we can check that they really are SMART by asking the following questions:

- Specific – Is the objective clear, precise, and unambiguous, e.g., "open up a new market for our goods in France"?
- Measurable – Does the objective say how success will be measured, e.g., "taking a 10% market share".

- Achievable – Is the objective realistically achievable considering the timeframe, resources and support that are available, e.g. there is scope to expand because market research shows that the market is growing at 20% per annum?
- Relevant – Is the objective relevant to what the business and/or the team need to achieve and in support the achievement of the overall goals of the organisation, e.g., because the 10% share will generate the return on investment set by key stakeholders?
- Time bound – Has a specific date been agreed for when the objective should be completed, e.g., "by the end of calendar year 2025"?

As with any process, monitoring and control is essential. A change process cannot be unguided else it will certainly run off course. It is necessary to assess performance against plan and to be prepared to change the means and the route while maintaining focus on the fundamental aims of the process. Equally importantly it is necessary to avoid paralysis by over control so there must be room for learning and emergent good practice especially in response to changed circumstances. This is, of course, all a part of good leadership. Performance should be assessed at least in relation to the following:

- Closeness to delivery of critical success factors
- Achieving milestones
- Adequacy of resource allocation
- Future resource needs
- Changes in external and internal environment
- Feedback from change agents

Successful implementation of strategic change requires clarity about the vision and the ability to lead people to change themselves.

REBECCA RAWNSLEY – A MODERN MANAGEMENT CAREER

Q I believe that you have often been involved in organisational change in your career, so what are your reflections on these experiences?

Firstly, every organisation is vastly different so tips and tricks that might work can be developed; but equally they may not turn out to be useful. It is important to have a very clear vision. So, I am working on thinking out some changes right now; I have my vision, I have all my detailed observations of my team, I know exactly what we need to do.

I am working with all the people to make sure they are ready, and to be sure I can take them with me. But I have got to think around what realistically can be done so that I can get my pitch very clear in my mind. I think those are the things that I have learned over time. It was often a stumble through to start with. You must get the right message to the right people, so that you have the support and buy in for the project, If the change needed is quite big you must manage expectations and not get carried away trying to do everything all in one go.

Q OK, a first piece of advice from you is that context matters, changing is different in different places and at different times, and so on. The second thing is planning, planning, planning, planning. Would the third thing be easy steps?

Yes, I think it is. It is about laying the building blocks and the foundations well, so you and your people get some success and do not become frustrated or scared by scale.

Q And another time there will be new factors at play in the new situation?

The situation is always different, and the people are usually different as well. So OK, so we've got planning, we've got context. We've got in a sense of softly, softly, small steps building up gradually.

Q Should you never try to jump straight to the end point, even if the matter is very, very urgent?

I think that in all circumstances you should really struggle to find preliminary steps. I think the knee jerk jump to the end point either works for a very short period or it just fails and fizzles. This can cause such damage. What, for example, would be the impact of the change outside the area for which the change was designed? What will be the impact of it failing completely? What about your own future credibility?

Q OK. If we are going through one of these change processes, whether it's big or whether it's small, you implied that it is all about people. So, what is it about people, because it seems to me that people are capable of almost anything. In the right place at the right time. So, what is it that makes change management difficult, do you think?

I think it is their internal drivers and their worries. Do they have any concerns? Has there been a recent round of redundancies?

Is the market in a bit of a downturn? Are they worried about losing their status? Personal disadvantages, personal negatives or maybe they feel they have been working really well so why is this needed or perhaps they realise how disruptive it is all going to be? I think it is generally personal concerns whether it's for their own role, their department, friendships that they might lose or whatever. Also, there can be a sort of change fatigue, a fatigue with disruption. Big organisations are always changing, and it's not necessarily always done very well.

Q Am I right then to suggest that very many organisations do not have the have the foggiest idea how to manage change?

Correct. Mostly, they just inform people. They tell people of things that are about to be done to them. That is annoying, anyone might ask why this was not shared with them before this? To do that would have given time to process it, to come to terms with it, to understand. Equally people might well feel slighted not to have been involved because typically, they would have had quite a lot of useful contributions to make. Of course, people can also be scared, hesitant or nervous about what the change will mean for them, for example the need to develop new skills.

Q One of the perennial dichotomies in strategic thinking is between planned and emergent change, i.e. change that just bubbles up from the day-to-day experience of people close to the work of the organisation. Often this indicates the best way to go. I wonder if this has been reflected in your experience.

Yes, gradually, over time, people realise they are working slightly differently now. They realise that this new approach is working well. It makes the changing that everyone must do much more manageable. Change becomes just a smooth transition. Over time the amount of change can be very substantial but without the pain.

THE CHAPTER EXAMPLE CASE – MEL

Developing the Change Plan

Sarah had to think through the change management implications of her strategic conclusions (Box 9.4).

Box 9.4 Key Things for the Leader to Address in Managing Change

- Communicating the need for change – acceptance of need will help a lot to overcome resistance to change.
- Communicating the practical changes and supporting adjustment processes – helping people to understand what is changing, why it is happening and how they will be helped to change themselves to meet new requirements will be important in easing the process of change.
- Enabling effective feedback from those affected – it is crucial that the leader can understand how the changes are impacting people and how they feel about this.
- Resisting growth of the grapevine – it is crucial to know what is being thought and said, privately, about the change process and then to act to correct misunderstandings.
- Building a base of support for sustainable change – if people change superficially but do not actually accept and support the changes made then the new strategy will never operate well and is likely gradually to revert to the way things were done previously.

Sarah started planning for change by constructing a Force Field Diagram, as follows, so that she could understand and evaluate the relative size of the drivers for change and the restraining forces with which she would have to deal.

Driver for change	Evaluation	Restraining force	Evaluation
1. Loss of reputation among key customers and consequent impact on sales	+5	1. Shortage of suitable highly skilled staff in the UK labour market	−3
2. Gradual move away from traditional motorsport to EV based motorsport	+2	2. Limited financial resources which are currently reducing as sales fall	−4
3. Ageing workforce threatening loss of key skills and knowledge	+4	3. Mid-career staff resistance to acquiring new skills.	−2
		4. Leadership team and product designers lacking knowledge of the proposed new markets.	−3
Total force for change	**+11**		−12

Sarah then asked herself whether she could see any ways to increase any drivers of change or decrease the restraining forces? She noted that the move from traditional automotive products to EV products was accelerating quickly across the automotive industry. She felt that she had to assume that this would apply also to motorsport. Equally it was clear to her that loss of reputation, if not stemmed by swift action would worsen to becoming irretrievable quite quickly. So, both Driver for change 1 and Driver for change 2 would increase in strength rapidly over time.

Turning to the restraining forces, she saw that swift action would reduce the impact of loss of sales on MEL's financial resources but resistance to developing new knowledge and skills and a lack of knowledge amongst key leaders and designers were more difficult to address.

Overall, she concluded that swift action, even if partial or to some extent misdirected, would be the right approach.

Sarah then moved on to assess each stakeholder group to see where they stood on the proposed strategy. She constructed a table as follows.

Stakeholder list	Relative power	Would actively oppose	Would not actively oppose	Would help to make the change	Would be a leader of the change
Senior Management Team/ Shareholders	5			X?	X?
Trade Unions	2		X		
Local community	1		X		
Customers	4			X	
Current suppliers	3			X	

This seemed to indicate to Sarah that her strategic proposals were pushing at an open door, but she had to admit to herself that she was unsure about the Management Team in this context. It was clear to her that they wanted to take action to regenerate the success of MEL and to sustain it into the future but, at the same time, she doubted that their knowledge of the new markets would enable them actively to lead the process of change except as figureheads.

Sarah concluded that there would need to be a change management process organised in such a way as to take advantage of the potential of the Management team to be figureheads while identifying change agents who either already had or could acquire the necessary knowledge of the new markets.

Thinking then of the change process itself Sarah applied the ideas of Lewin (1952) and the Three Phase Model in which it is recognised that the key changes to be made and the only ones that really are difficult in the end are those around people and their attitudes.

Phase 1: **Unfreeze** current attitudes – recognising the need to change, even if that need is disliked will enable a change to occur

- Sarah thought it probable that staff at MEL, especially those in direct contact with customers, understood that things were not going well. It would be necessary to build on this, ensuring that this knowledge was widespread, but also ensuring that staff realised that a plan had been formed to address the problem and that there was no obvious alternative other than planned decline.

Phase 2: **Move** to a new situation – the typical approach is to identify a series of steps which, taken together will achieve the overall change. The first of these steps should be relatively small and easy to accomplish to offer early wins to be celebrated.

- The chosen strategy was already constructed in the form of a series of steps. The first of these "detailed investigation and then correction of the immediate causes of poor performance at operational level" was indeed a relatively small and obviously appropriate response to the drop in sales and loss of reputation.
- Sarah recognised that she would need to construct a detailed plan for the implementation of the whole strategy step by step. In the case of each of the steps, it would be necessary for her to do the following:

  - Explore alternatives.
  - Identify specific obstacles to change.
  - Decide on a detailed change plan.
  - Implement plan paying special attention to people aspects.
  - Monitor progress and make corrections to details.

- It would also be necessary she knew, to build confidence and motivation for further change by celebrating success in an ongoing and comprehensive campaign of staff communications. An important part of enabling the new situation to be maintained would be to demonstrate that the new situation was indeed better for the organisation and employees, communicating success to all through good news stories.

Phase 3: **Refreeze** attitudes in the new situation – take steps to ensure that the changes achieved are sustainable and now represent the new working norms becoming part of the Organisational Culture. –

- The changes in staff and markets required by the implementation of the strategy would necessarily result in significant cultural change within MEL but there would continue to be a large proportion of the staff who were part of the old culture so that refreezing the new working attitudes would be very necessary to ensure maximum impact from the new strategy. The Senior Management team might in this context be a specific problem to be dealt with.
- As with any process, monitoring and control would be essential. It would be necessary to assess performance against plan. Equally it would be important to avoid paralysis by over control, Sarah knew that she must leave room for learning and emergent good practice especially in response to changed circumstances as new staff and new markets had their impact on MEL.

Sarah was now able to present her plan to the Senior Management Team. She asked for the immediate go ahead. This was approved and she was given the role of Change Manager and allowed to recruit a Change Agent from within each area of MEL. They would act under her control as local change managers implementing the agreed changes, following thorough local consultation, and feeding back to Sarah on the progress they were making.

KEY STEPS TAKEN AND OUTCOMES

Firstly, change agents were selected. Among the group, Sarah chose one to help her ensure that the new strategy was implemented successfully from a quality point of view across the whole firm. The chosen agent's background at BMW and its reputation for automotive quality had been a key part of his successful job application and established credibility in this field. He said that he was aware of a real difficulty among his colleagues in the Quality Team. He thought that there must have been indications that the team could have acted upon at a much earlier point, more forcibly alerting more senior management of the need to take corrective action (he was aware that regular reports were provided but they seemed to have had little impact). Why had the team not asked more questions and sought to press the need for action directly on their Director, Joe Coles? It was felt that there was a real sense of demotivation, how else to explain the fact that the team had allowed quality performance gradually to slip until customers felt they were no longer well served? It was essential that this was addressed if the new strategy was to be deployed successfully.

Secondly, Sarah had noted the problem around a lack of new blood and a lack of sources of new ideas in MEL. This was especially the case in Production and in the Management team too. Reflecting upon this she saw that a reorganisation could set up a situation in which new people could naturally become involved in management. But this would not be enough to address the lack of new thinking in the Production area of MEL. So, she proposed a programme of remedial recruitment designed to lower the average age while maintaining by knowledge transfer, the depth of knowledge and experience inherent the older members of staff before they retired. A first element of this expensive investment would be for Sarah to seek input on from an HR specialist to act as a consultant change agent to her change project.

Turning to the organisation of MEL, Sarah realised that a redesign of MEL was going to be an important part of the plan to implement the new strategy. This could retain the current simple functional structure, but she had noted three key areas in which organisational redesign was necessary:

- Business development was a specialist task which would need to have some effort devoted directly to it.
- Rebuilding of MEL's reputation among existing customers would likely fail unless the visibility and role in the culture of MEL of quality in general and the quality team in particular was enhanced.
- Bringing in some new management thinking via creation of a new senior quality role, Head of Quality Services reporting to the management Team now reconstituted as the Board of Management of MEL.

Sarah knew that the culture change required at MEL would not follow from some sort of management edict, she needed to create an internal movement that would spread recognition of the need for new attitudes and values around every aspect of the activities at MEL. The changes and investments mentioned above would demonstrate the seriousness of the management team, but it would be important also to take some immediate operational steps to show that MEL was conscious of the concerns being felt by customers and was prepared to tackle the underlying problems head on.

Did it work? Who knows, it is a story so let us say yes. But what is quite likely is that things will have gone less well and taken more time and effort than Sarah hoped. Meanwhile the world is moving on, competitors are strengthening, drivers of change in the macro environment are gathering strength, new challenges for MEL will be emerging. That is Management. Change, is a continuous thing; it is the source of all opportunity and threat. **Management *is* the Management of Change**

CHAPTER CASE – CHANGE AT MEDINSTANT

You are the new Senior Call Centre Supervisor at MedInstant.

MedInstant is a growing organisation based loosely in the not-for-profit sector.

It began life as a small call centre handling calls from 'life saver' medallions worn by individuals at risk in their own home, e.g., the elderly or frail. Calls were routed automatically to the Ambulance Service. As the organisation grew the call centre became more diversified handling calls from a variety of organisations linked into its call routing systems.

With the growth of the advice services funded by the Government such as providing instant medical advice by phone, calls are now no longer routed automatically but answered by a growing group of specialist advisors.

Growth is ongoing and MedInstant is now facing the challenge of that growth – to install a new IT system to handle the projected growth in volume of calls ...or not?

MedInstant's overall mission is to provide a specialist immediate response call centre service to any sector anywhere in Europe.

The organisation is now based in the Netherlands.

You have been in post about six months and it is clear that the work of MedInstant is growing faster than the capability of their existing technology. Senior Management has decided to install a whole new IT system capable of faster call handling. There is a rumour going round that not only will calls come in quicker but in order to pay for the system calls are going to be handled quicker by fewer staff. You have no idea if these rumours are true but have sensed a negative 'atmosphere' around the place.

Management seems concerned to ensure that the system will work and that a higher inflow of calls will net them a bigger share of the call-handling sector when they bid for new markets.

MedInstant's contract with the Dutch Government comes up for renewal next year and they are aware that they must be seen to be delivering in key results areas. It was founded on public sector type values – i.e. a commitment to staff retention and wherever possible no redundancies. So the Union is strong at MedInstant and has good relations with Management. However, over the last two years Union leaders have sensed a slow drift to private sector type working arrangements, which gives them some concern especially with regards to the rumours which are circulating about higher call turn-rounds and the possibility of fewer staff.

But the figures show that once the IT system is in place, even with quicker call turnarounds more staff will be needed in the next six months. A key question for Management is – should staff be told this? If so, when?

MedInstant's reputation rests very much on the people who handle calls – to demotivate them could be problematic for MedInstant. Also, the organisation does not pay the highest rates for call centre staff, currently they are linked Local Government pay scales. Already three excellent experienced staff have left to join the private sector on significantly higher salaries.

In terms of the proposed change, you have discovered from talking to the Call Centre Manager that it is true that the IT system is very expensive and also that MedInstant is regarded as doing a great job as it is and it is on target to keep the Dutch Government contract.

Tellingly, no other call centre has installed this new IT system anywhere in Europe but in the United States where it was developed, it is rated very highly as 'leading edge' technology. You wonder to yourself "Is this change for the sake of it?"

Source: based on the Author's practice.

CASE DISCUSSION QUESTIONS

The Call Centre manager has just been through an extensive management development programme which included an exploration of management ideas to do with Change. She has asked you if you would like to help her in working through this proposed change.

You find a quiet area in the building and begin to try to make sense of the change.

- **Task 1**

    Draw a Force Field analysis based on the information given in the Scenario for the proposed change. It may help to list the key stakeholders, the drivers for change and resisting forces before you begin to draw out your final diagram.

- **Task 2**

    How might you overcome their resistance – what is your preferred strategy? Why do you think it will work? Will all stakeholders/resisters need the same strategy?

CLASS DISCUSSION QUESTIONS

1. Explore how organisational diversity might impact a planned change.
2. What are the risks in seeking to make major changes just to a part of an organisation?
3. Can organisational culture be changed?
4. What is the relevance to a change manager of the urgency of the situation driving the change?

CHAPTER SUMMARY

- Change is a permanent feature of organisational life. Change in the external environment presents threats but is the origin of all opportunity. Changing is essential therefore, there can be no organisational "steady states".
- Change is really about people, all else is trivial. It is difficult to control and most likely there will be people who resist the change.
- The overall context for change must be and the driving and restraining forces can be analysed in terms of a *forcefield analysis*.
- *Levers* for managing strategic change include building a compelling case for change, challenging the taken for granted, changing operational processes, routines and symbols, political processes, timing and quick wins.
- There are many different types of change situation, but these can be thought of in terms of the *extent* of change required and its *urgency* – whether it can be achieved through incremental change and consultative processes or requires immediate action and a directive approach. Styles, and means of change need to be tailored to the context of the change.

- All management *is* the management of change (else it is administration). People follow leaders and leadership *is* the key to success in the management of change. In particular, the change manager leads a team of change agents responsible for local implementation and feedback to the change manager.

NOTES

1 Elsworth, T. (2024) *Understanding Strategic Analysis*, Abingdon: Routledge.
2 Balogun, J., Hope Hailey, V. and Johnson, G. (1999) *Exploring Strategic Change* (1st Ed.), Saddle River, NJ: Prentice-Hall.
3 Lewin, K. (1947) Frontiers in group dynamics: Concept, method and reality in social science; equilibrium and social change. *Human Relations*, 1(1): 5–41.
4 Kotter, J. (2012) *Leading Change*, Brighton, MA: Harvard Business Review Press.
5 Adapted from Reiss, G. (2007) *Project Management Demystified* (3rd Ed.), London: Taylor & Francis.

10 Worked Example – Major Change at Beamingly Holiday Holdings Ltd.

The case set out below (BHHL) is intended to offer a helpful, albeit imaginary, context in which readers can base their thinking about the material in this book and especially about the management of change. Readers, either individually or in class discussion, are encouraged to consider how Karl, our imaginary manager, sets about undertaking the task of applying material from Chapter 9 to his company.

BEAMINGLY HOLIDAY HOLDINGS LTD (BHHL)

Beamingly Holiday Holdings Ltd grew from a single, family owned, hotel in the beautiful Northumbrian seaside town of Beamingly. Through the second half of the 20th century and into the early years of the 21st century, it grew to encompass three other businesses in the same village, a café, a gift shop, and a caravan site just outside the village. Having achieved this size and range of services it was now the dominant player in Beamingly itself and held a significant share of the market in a radius of 10 miles.

In early 2018, BHHL was acquired by the Holiday Hotel Group (HHG, see below for more information). The former family owners of BHHL retain no interest in the company.

It is now October 2019. Earlier this year, HHG was reviewing strategy in the light of all its investments and as part of this broader review, it investigated BHHL and sought recommendations for its future development. This task was given to Karl Garcia who was then a recent recruit to the HHG following successful completion of an MBA at a prestigious European institution. Karl had a background in hotel management in the United Kingdom, France, and Spain.

DOI: 10.4324/9781032686592-10

Karl's first step had been to discuss the project with the Strategy Director of HHG to clarify the Group's wishes as the owners of BHHL. The Strategy Director pointed out that HHG had made a significant investment in BHHL and so they now wished to be advised how best BHHL might be developed in relation to its existing strategic position and in terms of BHHL contributing to the overall corporate success of HHG.

OUTLINE OF THE HOLIDAY HOTEL GROUP

The Group operates 30 boutique hotels (defined as a type of hotel that feels small, intimate, and quaint and stays true to its local culture). They are all aimed at touring/short-stay and weekend holiday-makers around England, Scotland, and Wales. All the hotels are in recognised areas of natural beauty which enjoy good tourist traffic all year around. Each hotel is run by a manager who lives locally. All the hotels in the Group are listed as three or four star and regarded as being positioned at the luxurious end of the tourist market. The Group has always been keen to invest in their properties to ensure that they retain this reputation, protecting the HHG brand, and it encourages the hotel managers, through profit sharing incentives (each hotel is a profit centre), to be intrapreneurial in their approach.

OUTLINE OF BHHL

HHG had not made any changes to BHHL since its acquisition. BHHL consists of four business units as set out below. Each business unit has separate accounts and is a profit centre although there is some sharing of resources, thereby rather confusing the details of unit profitability.

The Bishop Inn – the Inn dates from the late 17th century during the period in which a Bishop-owned Beamingly castle. It has a bar, a lounge, a restaurant offering homemade specialties from Northeast England and 20 double bedrooms, all of which are en-suite. There are also four family rooms, also en-suite, which sleep four. The bar and restaurant are open to non-residents. The Inn was last refurbished throughout in 2012 but all the public rooms were redecorated in late 2018. It is rated three star and is the most expensive accommodation and restaurant in Beamingly and its immediate environs. Most of the customers are from the United Kingdom with the occasional international tourist, usually from the United States, Canada, Australia, or New Zealand. These visitors are believed usually to be touring the United Kingdom and en route to or from Scotland.

The Cricket Pavilion Café/Bar – located immediately below the castle walls and overlooking the village cricket ground to the front and with beach and sea views from the terrace at its rear, this café and bar is popular with both locals and holiday makers. It serves locally sourced organic food from 10:00 to 21:00 every day. Prices are set at around the average for Northumberland.

Bishop's Gifts – this small gift shop is in the town main street a short walk from the Inn. It offers a range of mass produced locally themed gifts plus locally sourced craft work of all types.

Castle Farm Camping – is located just outside the village with access from the main road. The farm offers a fixed and touring caravan and camp site and upmarket glamping in shepherd's huts. While the camping and caravanning offer is at around the average price for Northumberland, the glamping is distinctly expensive, comparable with ordinary hotel rooms elsewhere in the vicinity. There is a shop/café which, as well as camper's essentials, also provides frozen homemade meals. Most customers are from the United Kingdom, but a small proportion are from Europe, principally France and Holland.

OPERATIONAL RESULTS FOR BHHL (PRE-TAX) FOR THE YEARS 2016–2018

Notes:

- VAT has been excluded from this data.
- BHHL owns all the properties from which it trades without mortgage.
- BHHL has no debt.

The Bishop Inn

VAT excluded	2016	2017	2018
Average occupancy rate	80%	75%	65%
Rooms revenue	£700K	£656K	£569K
Restaurant and bar revenues	£200K	£210K	£240K
Housekeeping costs	£100K	£102K	£104K
Building maintenance costs	£10K	£11K	£30K
Administration and Management costs	£50K	£51K	£52K
Restaurant and bar purchases	£30K	£33K	£40K
Kitchen, restaurant, and bar costs	£70K	£77K	£84K

The Cricket Pavilion Café/Bar

VAT excluded	2016	2017	2018
Café/bar revenues	£66K	£68K	£69K
Building maintenance costs	£2k	£2k	£3k
Administration and Management costs	£12k	£13K	£14K
Café/bar purchases	£10K	£11K	£12K
Kitchen and café/bar costs	£20K	£22K	£22K

Bishop's Gifts

VAT excluded	2016	2017	2018
Sales	£200K	£210K	£220K
Cost of sales	£66K	£70K	£72K
Building maintenance costs	£3k	£4k	£5k
Sales, Administration and Management costs	£60K	£65K	£65K

Castle Farm Camping

VAT excluded	2016	2017	2018
Average occupancy rate	75%	75%	80%
Camp site revenue	£50K	£55K	£60K
Shop sales	£30K	£35K	£37K
Shop, cost of sales	£10K	£12K	£13K
Site maintenance costs	£2K	£2K	£2K
Sales, Administration and Management costs	£10k	£12K	£13K

OVERALL BHHL RESULTS

Operating Profit	2016	2017	2018	Comments
The Inn	£630K	£580K	£486K	23% decrease
The Café/bar	£20K	£20K	£18K	10% decrease
The gift shop	£71K	£71K	£78K	10% increase
The campsite	£58K	£64K	£69K	19% increase
Total BHHL	£779K	£735K	£651K	16% decrease, approx. 5% decrease per annum

REVIEW OF BHHL RESOURCES

- Physical Resources

  - BHHL owns outright all the properties from which it trades.
  - Bedrooms in the Inn were refurbished in 2012 and all the public rooms were redecorated in 2018.
  - The café/bar was refurbished last in 2015 and the gift shop in 2013.
  - A range of IT and related equipment, mostly point of sale, leased.
  - Three fixed caravans to let and facilities for ten touring caravans and ten family size tents as well as three "shepherd's huts" style glamping facilities on the camp site. The three fixed caravans are approaching the end of their useful life, but the shepherd's huts were purchased in 2018 and are regarded as having a life of at least ten years.

- Human Resources

  - 21.5 full time equivalent staff including:

    - Administration, four full time equivalents, the Company Secretary (John McInnes) has a part time assistant/bookkeeper, the Inn has a night porter and a receptionist, the three other units have a part time bookkeeper each.
    - Kitchen staff, 2.5 full time equivalents, the Inn has a chef and a sous chef who also supply the café/bar where there is also a part time sous chef.
    - Serving staff, six full time equivalents, a barman at the Inn and one at the café/bar and eight part time waitresses at the Inn's restaurant and the Café/bar. There were also three part time shop assistants.
    - Cleaning staff, four full time equivalents, The Inn is cleaned by a team of eight part time cleaners who also have responsibility for the café/bar.
    - Management, 4, the management team is headed by the General Manager (James Smith, shortly due to retire), there is a hotel manager (Sharon Bates, also responsible for the camp site) and a restaurant/bar manager at the Inn (Ivan Thomas, also responsible for the café/bar) and a shop manager (Evelyn Barrat), at Bishop's Gifts. There is no marketing or sales function as such.

- Financial Resources
  - Cash at bank £0.25M
  - Significant asset base
  - No debt
- Intellectual Resources
  - Reputation of the Bishop Inn and of Beamingly itself, as a quality holiday destination.

KARL'S FINDINGS FROM HIS REVIEW OF THE CURRENT SITUATION

Karl assembled a group of colleagues from across HHG and BHHL to act as a sounding board for his thinking. At his first meeting with them, they discussed his findings from a general review of the current situation. They agreed on a statement of this which was as follows:

1. Physical Resources

   a. The Inn is well maintained but the rooms may be becoming tired and rather dated in design and layout compared with more recently established or refurbished hotels at other tourist locations.

   b. Both the café/bar and the shop are likely to need refurbishment soon.

   c. The fixed caravans at the camp site need to be replaced soon.

2. Operations

   a. Beamingly is a great holiday location, BHHL should prove, in principle, to be a high performing acquisition for HHG.

   b. Absolutely excellent service made up for almost any failings, but there was no doubt that there was a significant shortfall in customer satisfaction, most likely attributable to an overall feeling of a lack of quality, a lack of value for money, especially at the Inn. Karl's own experience in hotels across several countries had given him the same feeling when he first arrived at Beamingly.

   c. James Smith admitted to having been quite concerned by the reduction in occupancy levels at the Inn. On the other hand, he also noted that covers at the Inn restaurant and customer numbers at the Café/bar were on the increase albeit gradually.

3.   Human Resources

   a.   Although the staff of BHHL is not huge the local labour market is rather limited in scope and there are many competing businesses of a similar nature across Northumberland so that some difficulty is faced in recruiting suitable staff.

   b.   Apart from James Smith and John McInnes, in general management roles, none of the other senior staff were able to focus on their main role as all of them had subsidiary tasks relating to the smaller business units in BHHL.

   c.   Many of the other staff were in the same position also.

4.   Marketing

   a.   There is an almost complete lack of sales and marketing expertise in BHHL.

   b.   The Head of Marketing for HHG had commented that, unfortunately, the Inn did not have any method for acquiring customer feedback and the gradual increase in restaurant and café/bar covers seemed not to be in line with information he had seen about the significantly increasing numbers of tourists visiting the area.

   c.   The BHHL operations were not branded as such, each business unit operated separately.

   d.   The business had no social media presence marketing and sales activity was confined to traditional advertising and support from "Visit Northumberland" the County website.

5.   Finance

   a.   A strong balance sheet overall but the amount of cash available would be limited unless some of the assets could be sold or let.

   b.   Annual operating profit falling significantly overall.

A few days later Karl was successful in asking the group to give their support to a note he had drawn up setting out conclusions on BHHL's current position for consideration by HHG. The key points in the note follow below:

1. In the context of the immediate environs of Beamingly, the resources of BHHL were unique when taken as a whole. However, each resource taken individually appeared to be little more than a threshold resource, necessary simply to be in the business, and some of these resources were becoming rather worn. What then might be the sources of competitive advantage to be built on this set of resources? Perhaps two elements were important to HHG:

    a. The ability to provide a complete, comfortable, high-quality holiday or short stay.
    b. The first-class attractions of the location are in competition with other similar destinations in Northeast England.

2. Value was being provided to customers, but this value seemed to be increasingly focused on the restaurant, the café/bar, and some aspects of the camp site all of which were performing relatively better than the accommodation at the Inn. This was out of line with HHG norms and would not, eventually, align with the HHG organisational culture.

3. Currently, there were no real local competitors to BHHL, it would be costly to build a competing hotel, but there were other businesses only a few miles away which could be developed to threaten the BHHL domination of the local tourist trade. So, if one focused on the local market within which BHHL competed directly, then current performance could, relatively easily, be worsened by competing new developments.

4. In broad terms, BHHL is well organised and appeared, based on its long-term success and growth, to have appropriate systems for the activities it undertook – but there were specific concerns around aspects of the human resources, the need for investment, marketing and customer service.

5. Overall performance decline was being driven by falling Inn room occupancy. Karl knew that occupancy rates at the Inn had been good in 2016, but the reduction in recent years was a worrying trend, and it was now falling behind industry norms. The concerns about the resources might well, he thought, lead to a worsening of this performance, and the same problem might begin to arise in the campsite.

6. Karl knew from his previous experience and from advice he had from the Head of Marketing at HHG that there was concern in the industry generally about the unknown impact of BREXIT and that online B&B seemed to be presenting an increasing threat to the traditional tourist hotel trade. On the other hand, the tourist market generally seemed buoyant.

7. Looking at the individual business units:

   a. **The Bishop Inn** – is the main hotel operating in its area and has the highest single market share in that market so it should be able to contribute significant free cash flow to HHG.

   b. **The Cricket Pavilion Café/Bar** – serves both holiday-makers and locals but in terms of market share for the services it offers it is roughly equal to several other cafes including on the nearby main road to Berwick also pubs and the bar at the Inn. Its contribution to HHG is not significant and it falls outside the HHG line of business.

   c. **Bishop's Gifts** – the position of the gift shop is very similar to the Cricket Pavilion, sharing the market not only with a couple of other local shops but also the sale of gift items by cafes. Similar conclusions to the café/bar.

   d. **Castle Farm Camping** – apart from the glamping, Castle Farm shares the market with a few, but basic, camp sites on other local farms. However, the glamping offers the basis of an opportunity to create a sustainable business which may allow HHG to enter the online B&B market.

KARL'S CONCLUSIONS AND RECOMMENDATIONS

Karl's conclusions, supported by his colleagues, were as follows:

1. It seems from the occupancy data that so far as the accommodation at the Inn goes, customers are increasingly less likely to buy. Differentiation in hospitality is achieved through quality and innovation combined with responsiveness to customers – but these seem to be areas in which BHHL needs to make improvements at the Inn.

2. Opportunities exist in international and eco-tourism and in development of an online B&B offer.

3. Castle Farm Camping should be developed in the direction of glamping.

4. The Café/bar and gift shop are peripheral and making little
    contribution to the business so that both are candidates
    for divesting and the diversion of the resources released to
    improvements at the Inn and the camp site.

STRATEGY CHOSEN BY HHG BOARD

The board of HHG approved the following set of objectives for to be
taken forward at BHHL:

*   Refurbish rooms at the Inn and the old caravans at the campsite
    and develop a service excellence push.
*   Develop glamping offer at campsite.
*   Divest café and shop to focus on tourist accommodation, staff to be
    redeployed to remaining units.
*   Develop existing staff and recruit to create a marketing capability
    and enable development of modern online marketing.

    *   Develop a new market around non-European tourists.
    *   Develop a new market around eco-tourism.
    *   Developing a new product around online B&B including
        purchase and refurbishment of a B&B facility.

Karl was appointed to manage this change at BHHL.

APPLYING THE MANAGEMENT OF CHANGE TOOLKIT

Now Karl had to think through what the change management implications of this were and to develop a detailed change management plan.
Karl had found that his proposals were pushing at an open door with
the HHG Board, but he had to admit to himself that he was unsure
about how the BHHL Management Team would react to his ideas.

Reviewing his knowledge of the BHHL Management Team he sought
to identify how each of them would react to the changes approved by
the HHG Board.

The Management Team is now headed by John McInnes, replacing
the recently retired James Smith. John McInnes had been Company
Secretary for 20 years before the HHG takeover. Then there is a hotel
manager (Sharon Bates, also responsible for the camp site) and a res-
taurant/bar manager at the Inn (Ivan Thomas, also responsible for the
café/bar) and a shop manager (Evelyn Barrat) at Bishop's Gifts.

During the time that Karl had spent looking into BHHL he had learnt
quite a lot about these senior positions in the organisation and about

how they were likely to feel about his proposed changes. Sharon Bates would likely be very positive about the refurbishment of the hotel rooms and the significant upgrade of the camp site facilities. Ivan Thomas would lose the café/Bar but enhancement of the catering facilities in the Hotel and the expected increase in trade seemed likely to sway him to a positive position also. On the other hand, the shop manager would be very concerned about the future, whether the shop would be closed or whether there would be a new owner hardly mattered, either way it would be very unsettling.

Karl believed that John McInnes would see the changes as very radical, perhaps as dangerous, and certainly as undoing most of the business development work that he had been involved with in the previous 20 years. He thought it likely John would be strongly opposed to his ideas. What was worse, Karl knew that he was influential locally and would be Mayor of Beamingly in the coming year. From what he had heard, discussions in the local pubs were broadly negative to the "incomers" and certainly there had been coverage in the local newspaper to the same effect. To help with organising his thinking Karl drew out a stakeholder analysis as below (Figure 10.1).

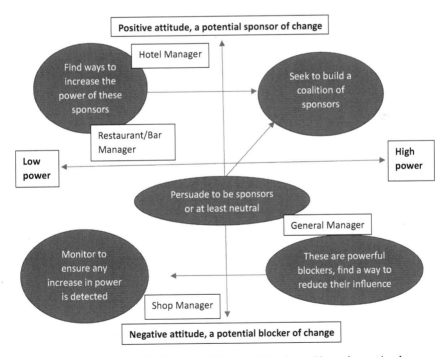

Figure 10.1 BHHL stakeholder analysis – positioning of key players in the stakeholder strategy model.

Bearing these thoughts about the attitudes of key stakeholders in mind, Karl reviewed his notes of all his previous discussions with colleagues and then started constructing a Force Field Diagram, as follows, so that he could understand and evaluate the relative size of the drivers for change and the restraining forces with which he would have to deal.

Driver for change	Evaluation	Restraining force	Evaluation
1. Rapid reduction in average room occupancy at the Inn	+4	1. Costs of refurbishment represent a significant proportion of income	−4
2. Need to refurbish rooms at the Inn and camping equipment at the camp site	+2	2. Existing staff lack expertise in key areas and recruitment expected to be difficult post BREXIT	−4
3. Limited nature of BHHL marketing expertise and limited nature of the markets accessed	+4	3. Mid-career staff resistance to acquiring new skills and resistance to changing roles and workplaces.	−2
4. Lack of congruence between BHHL activities and HHG norm	+1	4. Management team lacking knowledge of the proposed new markets.	−4
Total force for change	+11		−14

Karl then asked himself whether he could see any ways to increase any drivers of change or decrease the restraining forces? It was clear to him that the haemorrhaging of room occupancy, if not stemmed by swift action, would worsen to becoming irretrievable quite quickly. Equally, the condition of the rooms and the old caravans would only worsen if not dealt with. So, both Driver for change 1 and Driver for change 2 would increase in strength somewhat rapidly over time.

Turning to the restraining forces, the costs of refurbishment could be met from the proposed divestment of the café/bar and shop. The staff difficulties would, however, seem to be much more difficult to deal with.

Karl concluded that his change management process would need to be organised in such a way as to take advantage of HHG resources of expertise while identifying change agents within BHHL who either already had or could acquire the necessary skills and expertise.

Thinking then of this change process itself Karl applied the ideas of Lewin's (1952) Three Phase Model in which it is recognised that the key changes to be made and the only ones that really are difficult in the end, are those around people and their attitudes.

Phase 1: Unfreeze current attitudes – recognising the need to change, even if that need is disliked, will enable a change to occur

- Karl felt that the staff at the Inn, especially those in direct contact with customers staying there, understood things were not going too well. It would be necessary to build on this, ensuring that this knowledge was widespread, but also ensuring that staff realised that a plan had been formed to address the problem in a positive way.
- The staff at the shop and the café/bar would be more problematic. He anticipated that they would all be able to be redeployed to the Inn and the campsite, at least in principle. But this would be a big wrench for some of them. It would be necessary to convince them that the changes made sense for their long-term future with BHHL and that BHHL would be a stronger organisation able to offer enhanced careers in the future.

Phase 2: Move to a new situation – the typical approach is to identify a series of steps which, taken together will achieve the overall change. The first of these steps should be relatively small and easy to accomplish to offer early wins to be celebrated.

- The chosen strategy was already constructed in the form of a series of steps. The first of these was to refurbish rooms at the Inn and the old caravans at the campsite and develop a service excellence push. This was indeed a relatively small and obviously appropriate response to the drop in room sales and the state of the old caravans.
- Karl recognised that he would need to construct a detailed plan for the implementation of the whole strategy step by step. In the case of each of the steps it would be necessary for him to do the following:

  - Explore alternatives.
  - Identify specific obstacles to change.
  - Decide on a detailed change plan.
  - Implement plan paying special attention to people aspects.
  - Monitor progress and make corrections to details.

- It would also be necessary he knew, to build confidence and motivation for further change by celebrating success in an ongoing and comprehensive campaign of staff communications. An important part of enabling the new situation to be maintained would be to demonstrate that the new situation was indeed better for the organisation and employees, communicating success to all, through good news stories. This would be especially important in the context of the proposed divestment and redeployment of staff.

Phase 3: Refreeze attitudes in the new situation – take steps to ensure that the changes achieved are sustainable and now represent the new working norms becoming part of the Organisational Culture. –

- The changes in staff, staff location, skills and organisational capabilities required by the implementation of the strategy would necessarily result in significant cultural change within BHHL so that refreezing the new working attitudes would be very necessary to ensure maximum impact from the new strategy.
- As with any process, monitoring and control would be essential. It would be necessary to assess performance against plan. Equally, it would be important to avoid paralysis by over control, Karl knew that he must leave room for learning and emergent good practice, especially in relation to enhanced service excellence and the development of new marketing techniques and new markets.

KARL'S CHANGE PLAN IN OUTLINE

Key things for Karl to address in managing change would be;

- Communicating the need for change – acceptance of need would help a lot to overcome resistance to change.
- Communicating the practical changes and supporting adjustment processes – helping people to understand what is changing, why it is happening and how they will be helped to change themselves to meet new requirements would be important in easing the process of change.
- Enabling effective feedback from those affected – it is crucial that the leader can understand how the changes, as they take place step by step, are impacting people and how they feel about this.
- Resisting growth of the grapevine – it is crucial to know what is being thought and said, privately, about the change process and then to act to correct misunderstandings.

- Building a base of support for sustainable change – if people change superficially but do not actually accept and support the changes made then the new strategy will never operate well and is likely gradually to revert to the way things were done previously.

Main lines of activity were identified each containing several subactivities. Karl planned to carry each of these through in parallel, within each phase, albeit on differing timescales.

Phase 1

Preparing the ground

- Brief the Management Team on HHG plans.
- Identify and recruit Change Agents.
- General Manager briefs the Town Council and local press on the reasons for change and what they will see happen.
- Change Agents communicate with all staff around the need for change, the plans, and the specific changes each would experience.
- Change Agents feedback to Karl and the General Manager.

Phase 2

Moving to delivery of the change
A. Improve facilities/products.
  - Refurbish rooms at the Inn and the old caravans at the campsite.
  - Build on the glamping offer at the campsite.
  - Purchase and refurbishment of B&B facilities.
  - Developing a new product around online B&B
B. Restructure BHHL
  - Divest café and shop to focus on tourist accommodation.
  - Café and shop staff to be redeployed to remaining units.
C. Staff development
  - Develop a customer service excellence training programme and implementation plan for Inn and Campsite staff.
  - Develop marketing related skills in existing staff and recruit new staff as necessary.
D. Improve marketing and diversify markets.
  - Develop modern online marketing to broadening the proportion of the existing market addressed.
  - Develop a new market around non-European tourists.
  - Develop a new market around eco-tourism.

Phase 3

Stabilising the new situation

- Change Agents monitor progress and feed back to Karl and the General Manager.
- Early and ongoing successes are identified by Karl and communicated to staff by the Change Agents.
- End of plan review of the new position, the General Manager briefs Town Council and local press.

KEY STEPS TAKEN

To launch the process, Karl decided to speak separately with John McInnes before calling a meeting of the Management Team to brief them on the remit he had from HHG. He was able to persuade John McInnes that the changes demanded by HHG were needed and were inevitable if BHHL was to continue to prosper to the benefit of the employees and the wider local community and economy. Karl was aided in this by the John McInnes' recognition that in the new organisation of BHHL, with fewer and less diverse operating units, his own position could be deemed redundant. He could see that it was not really essential that there be a General Manager of BHHL as certainly, the Hotel Manager and the Restaurant /Bar Manager could with relative ease be managed directly by HHG HQ. Also, he had always been a committed BHHL employee and so he was willing to throw his weight as both senior manager and a leader of the local community, behind the changes proposed.

In a small business like BHHL it would likely only be members of the existing management team who had the breadth of knowledge and management skills to enable them to be Change Agents. Discussing matters with the Hotel Manager and Restaurant /Bar Manager, Karl discovered that his previous assessment of their points of view was correct, and he was easily able to recruit them to assist him in the role of Change Agents. Together they worked out a detailed communication plan for the briefing of all staff.

John McInnes, accompanied by Karl, met at the earliest opportunity with the Town Council and provided a press release and an interview opportunity, to the local press. It seemed that Karl was in luck, the local community easily recognised the local benefits of an improved tourist trade even if there was some upset and there were concerns in relation to the divestment of the shop and the café/bar. It was proposed, to general acclaim, that the Town Council should explore, with HHG support, ways in which the shop and café/bar might continue to operate as community-owned businesses.

As Karl had suspected, the member of the Management Team most concerned about the changes was Evelyn Barratt, the Shop Manager. The staff of the shop, three part time shop assistants, could perhaps be redeployed to the Inn or the campsite, but there was no obvious role for Evelyn Barratt. However, the news from the discussions at the Town Council was seen to be somewhat reassuring, Evelyn felt that she could perhaps play a leading role in the proposed new community-owned shop.

The refurbishment part of the changes was simply an operational matter and was indeed a relatively small and obviously appropriate response to the drop in room sales and the state of the old caravans. Karl was able to make use of specialist services provided by a contractor already having a well-established relationship with HHG. The development of customer service excellence depended on delivery of significant levels of staff training and then careful review and subsequent modification of all customer-facing processes. Again, HHG had an existing supplier well versed in these operational matters.

A start was made on all this but the visible improvement in facilities would act usefully as a first step which could be celebrated both internally and publicly rather early in the whole change implementation. This would also be an important part of enabling the new situation to be sustained long-term thus communicating success to all through good news stories. But most importantly it would be crucial to demonstrate that the new situation was indeed better for the organisation and employees, generating motivation to take on board the changes and make them a success.

In the end, Karl knew, it is the followers that do the work and make the organisation effective, not the leaders. The followers will do this if, as in this case, it is evidently to their collective overall benefit.

Index

Note: *Italic* page numbers refer to figures and page numbers followed by "n" refer to end notes.

9781032686615